24 discussion-starting sketches on teenage sexuality and God

GOOD SEX DRAMA

Jim Hancock

GRAND RAPIDS, MICHIGAN 49530
www.zondervan.com

Good Sex Drama: 24 Discussion-Starting Sketches on Teenage Sexuality and God

Copyright © 2002 by Youth Specialties

Youth Specialties Books, 300 S. Pierce St., El Cajon, CA 92020, are published by Zondervan, 5300 Patterson, S.E., Grand Rapids, MI 49530.

Library of Congress Cataloging-in-Publishing Data

Hancock, Jim, 1952-
   Good sex drama : 24 discussion-starting sketches on teenage sexuality and God / Jim Hancock.
     p. cm.
   ISBN 0-310-24547-8
   1. Sexual ethics for teenagers—Study and teaching. 2. Sex—Religious aspects—Christianity. 3. Drama in Christian Education. 4. Church work with teenagers. I. Title.

HQ35 .H347 2002
241'.66'0712—dc21

2002016761

Unless otherwise indicated, all Scripture quotations are taken from the *Holy Bible: New International Version* (North American Edition). Copyright © 1973, 1978, 1984 by International Bible Society. Used by permission of Zondervan.

All rights reserved. No part of this publication may be reproduced, stored in a retrieval system, or transmitted in any form or by any means—electronic, mechanical, photocopy, recording, or any other—except for brief quotations in printed reviews, without the prior permission of the publisher.

Web site addresses listed in this book were current at the time of publication. Please contact Youth Specialties via email (YS@YouthSpecialties.com) to report URLs that are no longer operational and replacement URLs if available.

Edited by Dave Urbanski and Vicki Newby
Cover design by Proxy
Interior design by Razdezignz
Photography by Jonathan Green

Printed in the United States of America

02 03 04 05 06 07 / VG / 10 9 8 7 6 5 4 3 2 1

Contents

Read Me: A Primer for Good Sex Drama 5

1. **Mango Sex** 11
   when and where and with whom sex makes sense
   monologue: Jules

2. **Fort Knox: Friday [Episode 1]** 15
   sexual disappointment and trust between friends
   dialogue: Jules and Knox

3. **Fort Knox: Insomnia [Episode 2]** 23
   trust and the results of sexual brokenness (eating disorders, isolation, cutting…)
   dialogue: Jules and Knox

4. **Fort Knox: Wake-Up Call [Episode 3]** 29
   trust and counting the cost of being honest about sexual issues
   dialogue: Jules and Knox

5. **Fort Knox: Baa-aah [Episode 4]** 35
   just how sneaky sexual temptation can get and what giving in does to relationships
   dialogue: Jules and Knox

6. **Fort Knox: Monkey See, Monkey Do [Episode 5]** 41
   pride, the point of no return, and unintended consequences
   monologue: Perry

7. **Coming Clean** 45
   technical virginity and telling the truth without being honest
   monologue: Warren

8. **Take My Breath Away** 51
   responsibility, gullibility, sexual storm troopers, and how sexually transmitted diseases spread
   monologue: Aryn

9. **The Volunteer** 55
   role models and honest answers to honest questions about sex
   dialogue: Ferne and Ginny

10. **Freaks** 65
    fashion magazines, double standards, and taking care not to cause the other guy to stumble
    dialogue: Jules and Ginny

11. **Vote of Confidence** 75
    the high price of free sex
    monologue: Ginny

12. **The Urge** 79
    sexual abuse and the temptation to pass it along
    dialogue: Warren and Nixon

CONTENTS CONTINUED

13. ONE MORE CALL 89
the responsibility kids have to look out for each other
monologue: Darryl

14. PROMISE ME: LATE NIGHT [EPISODE 1] 93
one girl's attempts to look out for her friend…with a twist
dialogue: Meliss and Billie

15. PROMISE ME: LET'S MAKE A DEAL [EPISODE 2] . . . 97
trustworthiness, truth telling, and the possibilities of do-overs
dialogue: Meliss and Darryl

16. PROMISE ME: AFTER THE FIRE [EPISODE 3] 107
do-overs and pledge rings
dialogue: Meliss and Toby

17. REPO 113
do-overs
monologue: Repo

18. OUT OF THE MOUTHS OF BABES 115
youth group sexual climates and personal responsibility
dialogue: Repo and Victor

19. ON A POSITIVE NOTE 121
sexuality and HIV
monologue: Victor

20. NOT THAT BIG A THING 129
sexual aggression and recovery
dialogue: Aryn and Caryn

21. W+S: LAMENT [EPISODE 1] 135
when role models fail sexually
dialogue: Sarah and Warren

22. W+S: GIRL TALK [EPISODE 2] 141
temptation and looking out for each other sexually
monologue: Sarah

23. W+S: WARREN SAYS HIS PIECE [EPISODE 3] 145
coming clean about sex
monologue: Warren

24. THE DREAM 155
putting sex in proper perspective
free verse: Jules, Warren, Ginny, and Repo

read me: a primer for *Good Sex Drama*

How to Use This Book

In *Good Sex Drama* you'll find a collection of sketches designed to generate discussion. They're snapshots of characters caught in a particular light, frozen in the moment when we bump into them. No one says these folks will end up where they are; it's just where we encounter them. So these short pieces don't end the discussion, they begin it.

There are two ways to perform each sketch:

- Reader's theater—actors read from the script.

- Traditional drama—memorized lines, props, staging, the whole nine yards.

Here are a few more ways to use these sketches. (Let me know if you think of others.)

- Use a sketch to illustrate a point in a talk or sermon.

- Use a sketch to open a Bible study.

- Use a series of related sketches to tie together three or five weekly meetings. (There's one series of five and two series of three.)

- Build a retreat around a series of related sketches.

- Ignore the recurring characters and cast different actors for each sketch. There are 16 characters, most of whom appear in more than one sketch. But the names aren't used much in the dialogue, so it should be relatively easy to present them as separate individuals (except Jules and Knox in the Fort Knox series).

- Write your own transition lines and make Warren or Jules (or any character you chose) a narrator who reminds the group what happened last time ("Last time, Sarah told Warren, 'blah, blah, blah.' Now we join Sarah the next morning.") or offers commentary on the characters' attitudes and choices.

- String all the sketches together (or choose a dozen) to create an entire evening of drama or reader's theater. (Let me know if you stage the whole thing. Maybe I'll come to opening night.)

Talk about It
Each sketch ends with a series of open-ended questions. The questions are designed to reveal what kids think and feel. Of course you'll use your judgment on this, but consider withholding your thoughts on the matter until the group has spoken. If you do, a couple of things could happen:

- At the very least, if you listen, you'll learn what's on the minds and hearts of your kids. Not a bad thing for a youth pastor.

- You may find the group exercising a teaching function even more powerful than your own—assuming there are people of conviction beside yourself in the group. (Oh, if you have other adults in the group, and if you intend to let the discussion run its course before you speak, tip them off to that fact. You're not trying to keep them from participating in the conversation, just from ending the conversation with a blanket declaration.)

A Word about Do-Overs
Do-overs. It's a term you'll run into several times in this collection of sketches.

Sooner or later, everyone needs do-overs.

People who use sex as a weapon and people who've been hammered with sex. People who make bad choices and dumb mistakes. People whose sexual experiments blow up in their faces. People who know Mr. Lust is a natural born liar but believe him anyway ("Hey, maybe this time things will be different"). People so arrogant or stupid they honestly think they're not like the rest of us. People consumed by thoughts of the next orgasm, and people consumed with pride because they've never had sex. People who wish they didn't know now what they didn't know then. We know who we are.

Everybody, sooner or later, needs do-overs.

But can we get them?

Children learn about do-overs in friendly games of hopscotch and marbles. A do-over is a second chance when someone makes a mistake. It's a gift between friends. No one has a right to demand do-overs. No one can just say, "Shut up! I'm taking do-overs."

A do-over is a favor, an act of grace.

A Word about Reader's Theater

If you don't have what it takes in time or experience to present these sketches as traditional dramas, please don't feel bad about treating them as reader's theater. You should still rehearse, you just won't memorize. I've seen marvelous reader's theater—so alive the audience couldn't have cared less that the actors were on script. I've also seen traditional performances that were DOA because the performers didn't have enough time to do them right. For our purposes, "doing them right" is delivering confident characterizations. If that means reading from a paper, do that with all your heart. (As if you needed permission!)

Why Use This Book?

May I tell you how it seems to me?

It seems to me that adults are *teaching* a lot more than students are *learning*.

This may follow the current inclination to believe our duty is done once we've said our piece. Unfortunately this inclination ignores most everything we know about communication, persuasion, and learning. (Does the teacher *really* believe her students heard what she thinks she said? Without a feedback loop, how would she know?)

But it explains why it seems, so much of the time, we're talking mainly to ourselves.

I think treating kids as passive listeners (or even note takers) rather than active, multisensory learners is a bad thing. It's something our Creator doesn't do.

> "Jesus spoke all these things to the crowd in parables; he did not
> say anything to them without using a parable" (Matthew 13:34).

The Son of God is a storyteller.

Jesus told stories, lots of 'em. Later—in private—he explained most of them to befuddled followers:

> "Lord, just a moment: Are you saying we'll be turned into sheep
> and goats when we get to heaven?"
>
> "Uh…not exactly."

Jesus used stories, questions, and monologues just about everywhere he went. And he seldom tied up the loose ends. Instead he left people to puzzle out what he really meant. That kind of stimulus and response generates thoughtful learning and decision-making. It's the kind of learning that sticks in a tough spot.

Let others talk *at* adolescents all they want. This book of sketches is a way to engage kids in conversations that engage them in learning that engages the way they think and the choices they make.

At least that's how it seems to me.

Meet the Characters

These 24 sketches involve 16 characters:

- six adolescent girls
- three adolescent boys
- four adult women
- three adult men

All 16 characters are linked to each other through relationships in the same community (though, if you perform each sketch as a stand-alone, no one need ever know that). Here they are, alphabetically:

• **Aryn** has herpes. She's lucky that's all she has. She's a sadder-but-wiser high school senior and a plainspoken and faithful friend.

• **Billie** is Meliss' mom. She only shows up once, but she sets up Meliss' character. As close as we get to a stereotypical, naive sitcom adult.

• **Caryn** is a bright, articulate junior, but she has a blind spot. She's foolishly trying to downplay the impact sexual misconduct has on her. It's not working.

• **Darryl** is an assistant principal who's sick to death of sexual craziness at school. Darryl is the administrator you'd most likely go to in a pinch. He's also Jules' stepfather and Ginny's husband.

• **Ferne** is Ginny's fortysomething friend. She's a little on the prissy side, though she means well.

• **Ginny** is Jules' mom and a volunteer youth worker. She's a reasonably cool middle-ager. She's married to Darryl.

• **Jules** is a sophomore girl who just wants to have fu-u-u-u-n. She's smart, funny, and uninhibited in ways that freak people out until they get to know her. Jules is Ginny and Darryl's daughter.

• **Knox** is a sophomore girl who went there, did that, and lost interest. As a consequence, she protects herself by keeping people at a distance.

• **Meliss** is a junior who's so busy with other people's business that she doesn't look at her own life very closely. She's good at misdirection and making mountains out of molehills.

• **Nixon** is a quiet sophomore boy with a dark struggle.

• **Perry** is an unremarkable sophomore boy who could blend into any crowd. But he chooses to not blend. He dresses in thrift-shop nerdwear to make the point that he's no slave to fashion.

• **Repo** is a junior boy with a tough reputation. He's also a changed man, working to leave his old life behind.

• **Sarah** is a bright woman who volunteers with the youth group. She's married to Warren, the youth worker; her age doesn't matter.

• **Toby** is a junior girl who's honest but not always direct—until she's cornered; *then* she tells it straight.

• **Victor** is a man in his 20s who volunteers with the youth group. He's HIV-positive and making the best of the rest of his life.

• **Warren** is the youth worker in charge. He's married to Sarah; his age doesn't matter. Warren is half comic, half prophet, and half Greek chorus. Warren has a thing or two to say about a thing or two.

These characters can change genders with a few alterations:

• **Aryn** could be **Aaron**
• **Billie** could be **Bill**
• **Darryl** could be **Dannie**
• **Ferne** could be **Frye**
• **Ginny** could be **Geoff**

- **Jules** could be **Jack** (but only in "Mango Sex")
- **Nixon** could be **Neela**
- **Warren** could be **Wynne**

If you feel moved, perform the sex changes as necessary.[1]

About the Format
The dramas are formatted in the screenplay style (with the speaker's name centered above the spoken lines) for one simple reason: in this format one page of dialogue translates roughly to one minute of performance time. That's a rough translation. If time is of the essence, rehearse with a stopwatch.
Here's how it looks on the page:

The outer margins are for **titles** and **general information**.

> **Stage Directions** are single indented from both sides. Most directions are brief and to the point. Embellish your brains out.

> > ### CHARACTER NAMES are centered.
> > (**Character Notes** are centered in parentheses)
> > **Dialogue** is double indented on both sides. This has the added benefit of positioning the whole block so it's easy to read without a lot of eye shifting. This seems to make dialogue easier to learn than the traditional stage play format.

> > The scripts are written for the _ear_ more than for the eye, so emphasized words are in underlined italics. (See that on the word _ear_?)

> IF YOUR ACTOR CHOOSES TO MAKE HER POINT WITH A WHISPER RATHER THAN A SCREAM, AND IF SHE PULLS IT OFF, MORE POWER TO HER. (SEE HOW THE MARGINS SHIFTED TO THE SINGLE-INDENTED LOCATION FOR THE PREVIOUS STAGE DIRECTIONS? NOW BACK TO DIALOGUE.)

> > Ellipses (that's three dots) signify a trailing off...

> > Sometimes ellipses are used...I guess you could say they're used...well, you might say ellipses are used to designate an uncertain pattern of speech...or something along those lines...

> > The em dash—the long dash that sets apart a phrase like this—is an interrupter, whether the character breaks his own thread—which has been known to happen—or has it snapped by his partner—

> > ### EDITOR
> > (interrupting)
> > We get it already! Move on!

That about covers format.

---

[1] The change may be hardest with Sarah and Warren. If a woman is in charge of your youth ministry, it may be awkward to present a male lead youth worker in the person of Warren. The simplest solution is change a few lines to make Sarah the lead youth worker and Warren her boyfriend, brother, best friend, or spouse, for whom she's nervous because she sees things he doesn't.

Stagecraft
If there's any magic to getting a troupe together, I don't know it. Of course, it helps having experienced people in the mix, but the only way to get experience is by *doing* it. So, if you haven't already gotten your group together...

I don't recommend beginning with a Big Production. That will take weeks at a minimum—more likely months—to produce. Big Productions can become all consuming. If you don't watch out, you find that *the play's the thing* (in a different way than Macbeth had in mind). It's probably not worth it.

Start simply. Find out who reads well and help them polish monologues or simple dialogues in reader's theater. Build from there. Spice your talks with drama. Replace them with drama; see if anyone misses your one-person show.

As the enterprise grows, add to it. Get some lights. They don't have to be complicated. I've rigged simple, inexpensive systems, and I'm an idiot about things mechanical and electrical. I've depended on stuff I bought at home-improvement stores: outdoor halogen lamps patched by extension cords into a simple dimmer box that a guy at church helped me build. Plug 'em in, and let the show begin.

To my amazement, every time I've gotten a drama team together, we've had as many invitations to perform as we've cared to pursue. Pieces we developed for adolescent audiences got us invited to perform for single adults, Sunday night church, for groups across town, even public schools.

We never forced it. Always took our time. Let God do what God does.

We also never told anyone they couldn't be a part of the troupe. Some had no desire to be in front of the audience and were delighted to work with lights and music. Others struggled to pull their dramatic weight but—and this is the beauty of writing and adapting material for a group—we always found something meaningful for them to do.

In some ways, the best part has always been building a crew and group of actors who depend on each other and on Christ and who want to help people. What's not to like about that?

What to Do if You Stir Up Trouble
If you use these sketches, *you're saying you're not afraid to talk about difficult issues.* And if you make your group feel the least bit safe in the discussion, there's a chance someone will come out with something shocking.

If that happens, you'll have to decide in real time how much you'll deal with right then and there—and what you think should be reserved for a more private dialogue after the meeting.

If a kid reveals troubling, frightening, even dangerous things about her sexual experience, *don't freak out.* Chances are if someone chooses to trust you with a difficult story about, say, sexual abuse, she won't go off the deep end any time soon. She's probably carried the story silently for a while, and you've given her the impression you can help. You can. You can't fix things, but you can help her get the help she needs. So take a deep breath, express your sympathy, and listen like crazy. And *don't freak out.*

If, after you hear a student's story, you believe a reasonable person would call it sexual abuse, chances are—and that's about 99 chances out of 100, so you should assume this applies to you—you're what most states call a *mandated reporter.* That means if you have convincing evidence of sexual abuse, the law requires you to report it.

If you're not sure how to do that, use one or more of these resources:

• Begin with the senior staff member in your church or organization. That person will probably know what to do. If you're convinced the situation is real—but your staff leader seems confused or you fear he will sweep it under the rug—take the next steps. (And remember, you're a mandated reporter so don't let anyone talk you out of speaking up—and into breaking the law.)

• Call the head counselor or vice principal at your local school—the one who's most sympathetic to kids. Ask her to help you understand your legal responsibilities. See if she'll interview the student involved (with or without you present) and help you assess the seriousness of the situation. In the (highly) unlikely event the kid is lying, the school official will be a good backup. Chances are, the counselor will be willing to call the sheriff, police, or Child Protective Services (or whatever it's called where you live). Law enforcement jurisdictions can be confusing, and it's easy to get lost in the system. School personnel have probably already been through this (more often than they wish); they'll walk you through it if you ask humbly.

• Get in touch with a trustworthy counselor or therapist and ask him to be a resource to you.

• If you go through all these channels and you believe nothing is happening, start again at the top, express your frustration humbly and directly, then ask for help. Be the widow in Luke 18 who keeps coming to the judge for justice until he pays attention—if only to get her off his back. (I know. I know. That's a parable about praying, so stop reading before you get the Big Lesson of the parable and just look at the story: a poor widow who harasses a powerful judge until he gives in. You're a poor youth worker looking for justice in a system where you probably don't feel at home. That's okay. Keep after it. They'll listen to you eventually if you don't give up. But don't showboat. Don't parade around city hall or call press conferences to put people on the spot. You'll get through the system by building relationships, not tearing them down. At least that's how it's worked for me.)

• Let your kids know about the Girls and Boys Town Hotline (800/448-3000). Girls and Boys Town offers a full range of help to callers—your students (and their friends) included. If you ask nicely, the hotline will send a stack of kid-friendly business cards.

• Childhelp USA specializes in helping those who've been sexually abused (800/4-A-CHILD).

• If you fear for a kid's safety and can't seem to get the help you need locally, you can call 800/NEW-LIFE (New Life Treatment Centers' in-hospital psychiatric program) for recommendations on how to proceed. New Life won't try to sell you anything and will give you the best information available.

There You Have It
Rehearse, perform, then ask questions that invite your group to think deeply about their lives. Remember: this is art, not science or theology. These 16 characters are growing from where they were to where they will yet be. Don't be mad if they say the wrong things. Instead, let them draw your students into conversations about themselves and their friends.
   And if it works for you, or if it doesn't, please let me know.

Jim Hancock

MANGO SEX

JULES is a smart, funny sophomore girl. She's uninhibited in ways that freak people out until they get to know her.

JULES SPEAKS VERY COMFORTABLY TO THE AUDIENCE.

JULES

Okay, I don't wanna get struck by lightning or anything but look—do you seriously want me to believe God would make something as cool as sex and then tell people to stay away from it?

I mean, really!

Because I find that hard to believe. I think that's like God saying, "Don't look at the mountains. Don't go in the ocean. Don't eat the apples."

Oh, wait, I guess that's the argument isn't it? That whole apple thing...

If *I* wrote it, it would be, "Don't eat the mangoes." You ever have a fresh, ripe mango? I gotta tell you: if sex is better than that, don't count on seeing much of me once I get started. I mean, please. Mango sex? I don't see why God wouldn't want that for everyone!

On the other hand, I hear about people—parents mostly, but people my age, too—who stop having sex. Which I find mind-boggling. That's like living in a mango...umm...what would that be? Mango ranch? Farm? Orchard? Orchard! It would be a mango orchard. Or would it be a grove? Okay, it's a grove. Giving up sex—once you have it, I mean—would be like living in a mango grove and not eating mangoes. Why would a person do that? Because it's just too good?

"It's just too much pleasure. I'm sorry I can't take it any more. Enough with the mangoes morning, noon, and night. Constantly mangoes! I'm fed up with the goodness! Bring me the arugula[2]. I want a meal of kale. No, no—no mango for me, I'll just have another helping of those turnips."

Or nothing at all. Is that the alternative? Is good sex really *good*? And is <u>no</u> sex better than bad sex? I heard my uncle say there's no such thing as bad sex. He calls himself a *serial monogamist*. I'm not clear about what that means, but he's never brought the same…uh…<u>guest</u> for Thanksgiving <u>and</u> Christmas. Last time he came alone. I'm not sure what that means, either.

Maybe people get discouraged because there's something wrong with the sex <u>they're</u> having, like, somehow, it's not ripe yet. See, that's interesting because I've only had ripe mango. Maybe unripe mango is a deadly killer. Or maybe it makes your mouth go all puckery.

I mean, everyone likes to say <u>*puckery*</u>, but nobody really wants the experience, right?

I think I have to explore this ripe mango theory.
"How will I know when the mango is ripe?"

"Don't worry, you'll know."

Really? I don't think so. I suspect there's more to it than that. I mean, "We will serve no mango before its time," right? Maybe that's true. Maybe until it's ripe, mango is just a pithy, puckery piece of fruit. Maybe it didn't even get the name *mango* until somebody learned the art of telling when it's ready to eat.

---

[2] A Mediterranean plant (Eruca vesicaria subsp. sativa) having flowers with purple-veined, yellowish-white petals and pungent, edible leaves.

And maybe sex is like that. "We will have no sex before its time." It has a ring to it.

I have a feeling the stakes are higher than choosing a ripe mango. Pick the wrong mango and what have you lost, really?

That's definitely not the impression I get from people who chose the wrong sex partner. I think I have more research to do. Meanwhile, I find myself with a powerful craving for…mango. Imagine that.

LIGHTS OUT.

discussion talk about it

Q: What about Jules' monologue grabbed you?

Q: What did she say that you agree with strongly?

What did she say that you disagree with strongly?

Q: Have you ever wondered why God seems to restrict access to good things like sexual expression? Talk about that.

Q: Do you think there's a difference between giving up sex and giving up on sex? Explain your thinking.

Without embarrassing anyone, do you know anyone who seems to have given up on sex?

Q: Have you seen serial monogamy work out well for anyone? Without naming anyone, tell us about what happened.

Q: Jules explores the idea that sex can be bitter fruit if consumed too soon. What do you think about that?

Fort Knox: Friday

[EPISODE 1]

JULES
is a smart, funny sophomore girl. She's uninhibited in ways that freak people out until they get to know her.

KNOX
is a mature sophomore girl who went there, did that, and lost interest. Knox protects herself by keeping people at a distance.

> **optional props...**
>
> **SLEEPOVER STUFF**
> 2 pillows
> 2 blankets
> 2 pairs of flannel pajamas
> 2 pairs of slippers
> stuffed animals
> snacks

          JULES
Don't tell me you don't wonder.

          KNOX
I don't wonder.

          JULES
You do, too!

          KNOX
I really don't.

          JULES
Shut up!

          KNOX
Fine.

          JULES
You wonder, Knox.

          KNOX
I don't wonder, Jules, and do you know why?

          JULES
Liar.

GOOD SEX DRAMA

KNOX

Because I don't care.

JULES

Liar.

KNOX

Fine.

JULES

Fine.

How can you not care Knox? Everybody cares.

KNOX

Not everyone.

JULES

How can you not care? I care. I wonder about it all the time.

KNOX

Well don't. It's a waste of time.

JULES

How can you say that?

KNOX

Because it is.

JULES

And you know this because…

KNOX

I know this, because…

JULES

Omigosh! What have you heard? You know something!

KNOX

Just stuff. Don't worry about it.

JULES

No, not fair! You have to say. You can't just start something and not finish it. You have to say. Who is it? No, wait! No names, just give me details.

KNOX

You're sick.

JULES

Yes, I am. But I'm about to feel much better, right? No names. If I can't figure it out, I don't deserve to know.

KNOX

I'm not gonna do this, Jules.

JULES

Sure you are. It's Friday night, there's nothing on television, we can't go anywhere…

KNOX

No good can come of it.

JULES

This is where you're wrong. I'm seriously considering finding out for myself, if you catch my drift. So you tell me about it, and I won't have to experiment. It's not like I haven't had opportunities.

KNOX

You're too chicken.

JULES

Before, maybe. But we're not gettin' any younger…

KNOX

Please. We can't even drive.

JULES
But we're old enough to wonder about driving aren't we. I mean, they give us driver's ed at school, right? They know we're gonna drive sooner or later. Right?

Don't you want me to be the best driver I can be? Don't you want me to know how to drive safely?

KNOX
Jules…

JULES
Knox…

KNOX
Don't mock me.

JULES
It's hard not to do, Knox. I mean, clearly, you want me to believe you know something, but you won't tell me what. You just want me to trust you. So, gimme a reason to trust. No names, just the details.

KNOX
Okay, look, I have a friend who gave it up, like, really young, and it caused nothing but heartache. She told me not to go there, and I believe her. Okay? Move on. Let's watch a video.

JULES
No. No. Nuh-uh. If you think that gets you off the hook, you are so seriously wrong. Who do you…what kinda…no ma'am. Not even close.

KNOX
Close as you're gonna get.

JULES
This is where you're wrong, Knox. I'm experiencing a lot of sexual pressure right now. I'm fightin' for my life.

KNOX

You're not serious.

JULES

Desperately.

KNOX

Is this Richie? Cuz I'll kick Richie's—

JULES
(interrupting)

Oh! Oh! Oh! I'm gonna be sick! How could you say his name in this conversation? We are so over! I don't even know you. You're a stranger to me!

KNOX

Oh, settle down. I just thought maybe he was coming around again. I told you he was a sleaze. If he does come around, you tell me and I'll crack his—

JULES
(interrupting)

Will you puh-leeze? What has got you all worked up? You're scary!

KNOX

Oh: Did I say that out loud? My mistake. What video was it you wanted to watch?

JULES

The one about you being all weird.

KNOX

I'm not all weird. I just don't wanna talk about this anymore.

JULES

You know they call you Fort Knox.

KNOX
They do not. They who?

JULES
They everyone. They say you have it locked up and surrounded by barbed wire.

KNOX
Well, good. If that's what they think.

JULES
It certainly frees up your Friday nights.

KNOX
This is a bad thing?

JULES
I guess not. Not if you choose it.

Okay, fine. You win. What video do you wanna watch? If Tinkerbell is on the box, I have it. If Eddie Murphy talks to animals, I have it. *Anne of Green Gables, Princess Bride, X-Files...*

KNOX
I'm the friend, Jules.

JULES
Yes, you are. Now whadaya wanna watch? You wanna make cookies? Split a bag of potato chips? Rob a convenience store?

Okay. I'm calm now. I heard you, Knox. I just had to... I don't want you to be the one who got hurt, okay?

KNOX
Yeah, thanks. Too late, but thanks.

JULES
Can you talk about it?

KNOX
Yeah. Well, before we were friends, a coupla years ago, I was all, like, so against the whole dating thing—

JULES
Unlike today, when there just aren't enough weekends in the month.

KNOX
Okay, so nothing has changed. Look, are you gonna make this hard on me?

JULES
No. Sorry. Maybe a little bit, if you say funny things.

KNOX
All right, fine. I've come this far.

JULES
You could turn back. You don't have to do this.

KNOX
Seriously?

JULES
No! Are you crazy? This is, like, this huge breakthrough in our friendship! I'll spend the rest of my life trying to be worthy of you. You can't turn back now! You've got me right where you want me.

KNOX
No, I really don't. If I tell you this…if I tell you this, I have to know you won't ever use it against me.

JULES
'K, now you crossed over to the dark side. Why would I hurt you? Have I ever hurt you? Ever broken your trust even a little bit? Have I?

KNOX

No.

JULES

Not even once.

KNOX

I never gave you anything you could really hurt me with.

JULES

Oh…I thought…look, if this is too far, go back now. This conversation never happened. I'm good with that. I just thought…I don't know what I thought.

I guess I never gave you anything all that real, either. I'm sorry I pushed. Excuse me, I hafta go to the bathroom.

JULES EXITS AND THE LIGHTS GO DOWN.

discussion talk about it

- **Q:** How would you describe Jules to a friend?
- **Q:** What do you think makes sex so intriguing to people like Jules?
- **Q:** How would you describe Knox to a friend?
- **Q:** No names, just details. Raise your hand if you know anyone like Knox.
- **Q:** On a scale of one to five, how much do you think Knox trusts Jules?

1	2	3	4	5
not at all, because…		somewhat, because…		totally, because…

- **Q:** What did you think when Knox said, "I never gave you anything you could really hurt me with"?
- **Q:** Where do you imagine this story is going?
- **Q:** What would you advise Jules to do now?
- **Q:** What would you advise Knox to do now?

Fort Knox: Insomnia

[EPISODE 2]

JULES
is a smart, funny sophomore girl. She's uninhibited in ways that freak people out until they get to know her.

KNOX
is a mature sophomore girl who went there, did that, and lost interest. Knox protects herself by keeping people at a distance.

LATER THE SAME NIGHT AS "FORT KNOX I." JULES AND KNOX ARE IN BED. KNOX SITS UP.

> **optional props...**
>
> **SLEEPOVER STUFF**
> 2 beds
> 2 blankets
> 2 pillows
> 2 pairs of flannel pajamas

          KNOX
Hey?

          JULES
Yeah?

          KNOX
You awake?

          JULES
I think so. Just a second. Yeah, that's me. Can't you sleep?

          KNOX
Not really.

JULES SITS UP.

          JULES
You're feeling bad about not telling me what happened, aren't you.

          KNOX
Not really. I'm feeling bad about what happened. I try not to think about it much if I can help it.

GOOD SEX DRAMA

JULES

And can you usually help it?

KNOX

Usually. Sometimes. Not really. No.

JULES

Is that hard?

KNOX

Pretty much, yeah. I do stuff to keep my mind off it, but that doesn't always work.

JULES

Like what?

KNOX

Oh, you know, the usual. Starving, then bingeing and purging, then starving again. I cut myself for while, but that seemed really stupid.

JULES

As compared to starving to death?

KNOX

I'm trying to be honest here. If you're gonna punish me, I can just shut up, you know. I mean, I know how to keep a secret.

JULES

Sorry.

KNOX

I know. I suppose it sounds funny.

JULES

Not really, Knox. It actually sounds kinda crazy. You know?

KNOX

Yeah.

JULES

You must've been hurt pretty bad.

KNOX

Yeah. It was…hard. It's still hard. If I could just walk away, I absolutely would.

JULES

But what? It follows you around?

KNOX

It has a way of finding me, yeah.

JULES

You know, they say talking about stuff like this takes away its power.

KNOX

They say that? Which *they*? The ones who call me Fort Knox?

JULES

The ones who try to help people. They say talking about what has a person locked up is like the key to…I don't know…getting out of prison. Sorry, I wasn't trying to make a metaphor, it just came out.

KNOX

Look, I'm gonna tell you what happened. You just have to promise me…

JULES

Anything. You tell me what.

KNOX

No, not anything. That's too big. *Anything* ends up meaning *nothing*.

You have to promise…you have to promise to *believe* me.

                    JULES
Whoa. Just how big is this?

                    KNOX
It's the biggest thing that ever happened. It's my defining moment.

                    JULES
Forever?

                    KNOX
I hope not.

                    JULES
Hey?

                    KNOX
Yeah?

                    JULES
Whatever it is, I'm sorry.

                    KNOX
Yeah. Hey, I think I'm gonna go to sleep now.

KNOX LAYS DOWN AND TURNS HER BACK TO JULES, WHO LOOKS AT HER IN SURPRISE AS THE LIGHTS GO OUT.

discussion talk about it

Q: What grabbed you in this exchange between Jules and Knox?

Q: What do you think of Jules' prison metaphor? Is Knox locked up?

Q: No names, just details. Raise your hand if you know people who abuse themselves by starving, bingeing and purging, or cutting themselves like Knox.

Q: Why do you think the stakes are so high following sexual disappointment that some people hurt themselves?

Q: What do you think Jules should do at this point?

Q: What do you think Knox should do at this point?

Q: Where do you think this story is going?

FORT KNOX: WAKE-UP CALL

[EPISODE 3]

JULES
is a smart, funny sophomore girl. She's uninhibited in ways that freak people out until they get to know her.

KNOX
is a mature sophomore girl who went there, did that, and lost interest. Knox protects herself by keeping people at a distance.

THE NEXT MORNING; JULES AND KNOX ARE EATING CEREAL.

optional props...

BREAKFAST STUFF
2 cereal bowls
2 spoons
2 juice glasses
milk
box of cereal
juice
table and 2 chairs

JULES
Are we okay?

KNOX
As far as I know. Have you heard anything different?

JULES
I haven't heard anything at all. It's like we broke up or something.

KNOX
That's ridiculous.

JULES
You're tellin' me.

KNOX
Look, I'm afraid I went too far last night.

JULES
You think you went too far by telling me you have something to tell me? That's too far?

KNOX
Well, what will your friends say?

GOOD SEX DRAMA

JULES

What friends? My friends are *our* friends. They won't say anything. They won't know there's anything to say. Look, does this all seem really weird, or is it just you?

Whadaya think? I can't wait to get you out of the house so I can tell people you have a dark secret but I don't know what it is but it must be really bad because you can't bring yourself to say it?

KNOX

Well?

JULES

You're a freak, Knox. I don't know how you could have made it any plainer that you don't want this story spread around than, than…

KNOX

By not telling it?

JULES

There you go. You *dumbfound* me.

KNOX
(laughing)

I what?

JULES

You dumbfound me. I'm…I'm *flummoxed*. I'm…

KNOX

Suessed?

JULES

What?

KNOX

You're Suessed. As in Doctor Suess. I don't know. You use words like *flummoxed,* and I think of Dr. Suess.

JULES
Where does this _come_ from? Do you sit around thinking of ways to...to...

KNOX
Flummox you?

JULES
Do you?

KNOX
I shut down last night because I was afraid.

JULES
Well that's fine, but I'm not the one you need to be afraid of.

KNOX
I know.

JULES
I don't starve you or overfeed you or cut you.

KNOX
I know.

JULES
And I don't talk about you.

KNOX
I believe you.

JULES
Well, I'm not comforted.

KNOX
I'm sorry.

JULES

So just gimme a minute to catch my breath and…aren't you supposed to be fighting back? Aren't you feeling attacked right now?

KNOX

No. You're right. I have it coming.

JULES

Well then, this is gonna be a short fight; that's all I have to say.

KNOX

Okay.

JULES

Okay then. So…whadaya wanna do now?

KNOX

I think I'd like to tell you a story.

JULES

Is this a true story?

KNOX

Yeah.

JULES

Okay then. I'd better get comfortable, right?

KNOX

I think that's a good idea, yeah.

JULES

You sure 'bout this? Because last time I took quite a beating, and I don't know if I wanna make you do that to me again unless you're sure.

KNOX

I'm sure, Jules. I'm sorry I didn't trust you, I just…I just didn't. It has more to do with me—and humankind—than you in particular.

JULES

I know. It's hard to know who's trustworthy. I get that. You take your time. It's your story.

KNOX

Yeah.

JULES DRINKS THE MILK FROM HER CEREAL BOWL AS THE LIGHTS GO OUT.

discussion talk about it

- **Q:** Talk about what grabbed you in this exchange between Knox and Jules.
- **Q:** Why do you think it's hard for Knox to trust Jules with her story?
- **Q:** No names, just details. Have you ever been in Jules position?
- **Q:** What would you tell Jules at this point?
- **Q:** What would you say to Knox?
- **Q:** Where do you think this story is going?

FORT KNOX: BAA-AAH

[EPISODE 4]

JULES

is a smart, funny sophomore girl. She's uninhibited in ways that freak people out until they get to know her.

KNOX

is a mature sophomore girl who went there, did that, and lost interest. Knox protects herself by keeping people at a distance.

IT'S AFTER BREAKFAST. JULES AND KNOX SIT COMFORTABLY, HUGGING PILLOWS.

> **optional props...**
> **HANGING OUT STUFF**
> 2 comfy chairs
> 2 sofa pillows

JULES

No way!

KNOX

Way.

JULES

Your best friend was a guy!?

KNOX

Why is that amazing?

JULES

Well, I don't know. It's just unusual. Were you guys, like, going out?

KNOX

We were 13; of course we weren't going out.

JULES

Thirteen-year-olds go out.

KNOX

Not with each other. Thirteen year-old girls go out with immature, older guys—

JULES
Hey! My brother went out with a 13-year-old—oh.

KNOX
Then you know exactly what I'm saying—

JULES
(interrupting)
So I know exactly what you're saying. There's no way the state should have trusted that boy with a driver's license. He was, he was…

KNOX
(interrupting)
He was immature. If that wasn't already obvious, it was clear when he fell for a 13-year-old.

JULES
Yeah, but she was a mature 13.

KNOX
Her mind or her body?

JULES
Eh…let's just say it wasn't her conversation that was stimulating—we're talking about my *brother* here. Oh, wait, we were talking about you. And your best friend was a guy, and of course you weren't going out—you were 13 years old. I'm back; I got it. Mind like a steel trap.

KNOX
Mind like a hard drive.

JULES
Fast and powerful?

KNOX
Random access.

JULES

But fast, blazingly fast.

KNOX

Nerd.

JULES

Freak…*Any*way…

KNOX

Dork…*ANY*way, we did everything together. By that I mean, we sat around the house doing nothing. It's just, we sat around the house every day for, like, two *years*, starting in sixth grade…watching TV and listening to music and hanging out.

JULES

Like we're doing today.

KNOX

Exactly. Just being together.

JULES

It sounds very sweet, actually.

KNOX

You know what? It was. It was really sweet.

JULES

Until…what? He turned on you? Turned into a guy or some awful thing?

KNOX

I wish it were that simple.

JULES

It could be. I'm prepared to believe anything.

KNOX
I know. It's just…more complicated than that.

JULES
All ears…right here in the sides of my head. Nothing but ears.

KNOX
What kills me is I didn't just <u>see</u> it coming. I brought it on.

JULES
Whoa, is this you saying, "I'm the girl; I should be the responsible one"? Because, if it is, I'm gonna hafta step outside to throw up.

KNOX
It's not that.

JULES
Then what is it? What did he do to you? How did he hurt you so bad?

KNOX
He didn't tell me <u>no</u>, Jules. He didn't stop me, and he didn't stop himself. He didn't say, "Hold on, let's think about this." He didn't treat me like a friend…

JULES
Knox, what part of "he's a boy" didn't you understand?

KNOX
I know. But honestly, we did it to each other. We used each other in a way friends wouldn't…in a way friends just <u>wouldn't</u>.

JULES
So, that part about being best friends…

KNOX
Not so much I guess.

JULES

So how did this happen...whatever *this* is...

KNOX

I mean, it's not like we ever *defined* ourselves as best friends or anything. We just acted like best friends...until we didn't.

JULES

And...

KNOX

It started out as a joke. We were making fun of people at school—it seemed like everybody was hooking up, and it was just ridiculous. Except...

JULES

Yeah?

KNOX

It was ridiculous.

JULES

But you were doing it too?

KNOX

We did it, too. We hid behind—at least *I* hid behind the sarcasm and abuse we heaped on the people we called *sheep*.

JULES

Baa-aah.

KNOX

Yeah, I mean, we started out mocking them for just doing what they saw on TV and movies. "*OH*," you know, "*OH*, so people our age are supposed to hook up. Okay, dum de dum dum." And we would pretend to have this messy kiss and then just crack up. And then we would just maul each other like people in movies until we cracked up again.

It was funny until all of sudden we weren't kiddin' any more, and nobody was cracking up.

JULES
Sounds like hooking up to me.

KNOX
Yeah, thanks. I wasn't sure.

JULES
Sorry. And that killed the relationship.

KNOX
Well, yeah. That and… oh my gosh. Jules? Don't you see where this is going?

JULES HUGS HER PILLOW AND SHAKES HER HEAD BLANKLY.

KNOX
Oh my gosh. I thought you *knew*. I thought you were just being nice.

KNOX RAISES HER FINGERS TO HER LIPS, AND JULES HUGS THE PILLOW AND THE LIGHTS GO DOWN.

discussion talk about it

Q: Where do you think this is going?

Q: What do you think of Knox's crack about immature boys and 13-year-old girls?

Q: What do you think about Jules' line: "What part of 'He's a boy' didn't you understand?"

Q: What do you think about Knox sharing the blame?

Q: Knox talks as if she was taken by surprise. Do you buy that?

Q: Seriously, if you've seen any really close male-female relationships that weren't ruined by sexual tension, we'd like to hear about them.

FORT KNOX: MONKEY SEE, MONKEY DO

[EPISODE 5]

"Monkey See, Monkey Do" finishes the Fort Knox series. If you choose not to perform episodes 1-4, this sketch stands by itself.

PERRY

is an unremarkable sophomore boy who could blend into any crowd. But he chooses to not blend. He dresses in thrift-shop nerdwear to make the point that he's no slave to fashion.

optional props...

HANGING OUT STUFF
thrift-shop nerd clothing

PERRY ADDRESSES THE AUDIENCE UNCOMFORTABLY.

PERRY

What's shocking is that we hooked up at all. I mean we're, like, best friends.

At least we were.

We used to hang out, like, every day after school. And all summer long. I mean, she had swimming and all, so that was a deal for a couple of months every year. And I had baseball.

Other than that, we were together just about constantly from, like, sixth grade or something. And it wasn't intense or anything. It was, like, "What're you doing today?"

And usually it was, "Nothing."

So, "You wanna do something?"

And it was usually, "No, let's just hang out."

And we would look at magazines, watch some TV—we had our little shows, you know. And we would, maybe, study or something. And then I'd go home. Or she would, if it was my house. And maybe we'd talk later if we felt like it. Which we usually did.

But not always, you know? Which is what was so cool. There was no, like, jealousy and stuff. We talked about that. We laughed at people who were all, "She's mine! _My woman! Ooga! Ooga!_" That's so lame. So…so…ape-ish.

I don't mind telling you we felt superior to…to everybody, really. Everybody was all pairing up at school, and we were, like, "Whatever." Like they were such sheep, and we were too cool for that. And in a way we were. I mean we didn't pair up. We just…I don't know how to say it.

One afternoon we just started fooling around…making fun of kids at school. It was funny. I thought we were just kidding around. I mean it was fun. I won't say it wasn't. And we made a joke out of it, like it wasn't sexy or something.

We did that a few times, you know, for laughs. We'd copy what we'd seen on cable, you know—not porn or anything; we weren't into that. But, you know, all in the spirit of the joke and everything, and we'd just be all over each other. Then one day we just kept going.

We didn't plan it, exactly. I mean I didn't plan for it to happen. But I didn't plan for it to not happen either. Neither of us said, "Okay, that's it. Game over. Zip up your pants." We should have, both of us. If either of us had said so, I know we would have stopped. I should have said something. What we had was too important for me to just go along.

Which is a lie. I didn't just go along. And it wasn't an accident, like, "_Oh,_ I tripped and fell out of my underwear!" I had to want it to happen. I mean, it wasn't that easy, you know?

So it did. I _wanted_ it to happen, and I can only believe _she_ wanted it to happen, so it happened.

After that, things got real weird between us. We both got real busy all of a sudden. You know, "What're you doing after school?" sort of thing. "Oh. I, uh, have this…this thing I have to do." You know?

And after a few weeks it was, like, tragic.

I mean, I know, technically, it's possible to get pregnant the first time you have sex. I mean, I _knew_ that.

There's a child in the world who has my DNA, but he's not my son. Maybe it's truer to say I'm not his dad. Sometimes I go a whole day without thinking about that. But not often.

I'm not his dad, and she's not his mom—and we don't know each other any more.

It was _so_ not worth it, you know? She was like my best friend… I miss her.

I truly do.

LIGHTS OUT.

discussion talk about it

Q: Talk about what grabbed you in Perry's monologue.

Q: No names, just details. Raise your hand if you've known anyone in Perry's situation.

Q: Where do you think Perry reached the point of no return?

Q: What would you say to Perry?

Q: Can this guy get do-overs? Talk about that.

If you need an explanation about do-overs, see page 5.

Coming Clean

WARREN is the youth worker in charge. He's married to Sarah; his age doesn't matter. Warren is half comic, half prophet, and half Greek chorus. Warren has a thing or two to say about a thing or two.

WARREN ADDRESSES THE AUDIENCE COMFORTABLY.

WARREN

I want to come clean with you about something. Okay? Is that all right with you?

Standing before you is living, breathing proof that it's possible to grow up in this culture without falling into alcohol and sex—please, hold your applause to the end.

I've never been drunk. People talk as if that's a rite of passage—something they do because they might as well get it over with…like it's inevitable. Well, it's not.

And the only person I've had sex with is Sarah, my lovely wife. Stand up, honey; let the people greet you. Sure you can clap for my bride. Isn't she beautiful? Yeah.

Like alcohol, sex is an experience about which some people say, "Well, I may as well just get it over with." That's too bad. Trust me. It's worth the wait. Every time.

People talk as if it were impossible to make it to adulthood without falling into that stuff—you know they do. Well it's _not_ impossible. I'm living proof.

I'll tell you what _is_ impossible. It's impossible to say the things I just said—in the way I said them—and be absolutely truthful.

Because everything I just said, while technically factual, isn't really true.

I learned very early in my drinking career that I have a high tolerance for alcohol. I found out I could drink a lot without showing any effects from it. I was one of those kids who could drink everybody under the table—people who outweighed me by 50 pounds couldn't keep up with me.

Now I know what you're thinking. A couple of you are thinking, "That would be so cool!" You know what? It was…for about a minute. Then I started learning about addiction. You know anything about alcohol addiction?

Addicts share three things in common. The first is they drink because they get something out of it; it works for them. They get some physical or social benefit from using alcohol that makes them want to drink more and more frequently.

The second thing about addicts is they _can_ repeat the behavior frequently because they have a tolerance for alcohol. It doesn't seem to affect them like it affects other drinkers. The problem is young drinkers tend to drink to get drunk, you know? I drank as much as I could as fast as I could because I had to be home by 11:30. Well, the amount of alcohol it takes to intoxicate an addict can be…well, I was gonna say _toxic_ but that would be redundant because it's right there in the word—_toxic_ is the root word in in_toxic_ate. And _toxic_, you know, means dangerous or poisonous. Alcohol poisoning can be deadly.

The third thing about addicts, is using alcohol starts to get them in trouble, but that doesn't stop them from using. They miss school or work, or they steal or lie or break relationships because they drink. Or in _order_ to drink. And they may feel bad about that, but they don't stop. In fact, feeling bad may seem like a good reason to drink.

Well, at 15, I had two out of the three. I could drink like a fish—that's high tolerance—and I got major props for drinking so much. That's the benefit that made me want to keep doing it more and more often.

Which I did, because I could. And because I got fame for doing it, I did it often. You see where this is going?

I'm one of the lucky ones—or maybe God was looking out for me—because I saw what was coming. I saw that, if I kept drinking, I was gonna turn out just like my father. Not good news to me. I shaved my head because my hair was so much like his. I started going to church because he wouldn't. I did everything I could to be different from my old man. Maybe <u>not</u> drinking was my little rebellion at home. Hmm…I'm gonna have to think about that.

Anyway, I stopped drinking before it got toxic. Seriously, I consider myself lucky…maybe blessed. A lot of people don't get off as easily as I did.

I don't drink today because I know where that leads for me. I may be wrong about that, but I'll never find out because I refuse to put myself at risk. It's not worth it.

So that's the truth behind the fact that I've never been drunk. Okay, that was the easy one. What I said about never being drunk was technically factual without being actually true.

The thing about only having sex with my wife? That's technically true as well, but…how to say this…?

I have this friend who had an affair with a man at church. He advised her on some problems, and she trusted him. He was…I don't know what was going on in his head…actually, maybe I do, and that makes me really uncomfortable…

Anyway, they got intimate. A lot. Over a long period of time—several years. It wasn't hard to come up with reasons to be together because they were at church, right? They were working on projects and reports and plans. It was easy.

And here's the thing. They never "did it." They never, technically, had sex if by that you mean…well, you know what you mean.

When my friend finally came to her senses, she was so embarrassed. She felt so foolish. "It was sex," she said. It was—I'll never forget how she said it—she said, "An orgasm is an orgasm. The fact that we didn't exchange body fluids doesn't mean we didn't have sex." If you don't know what that means, you can ask your neighbor afterward; I'm sure he or she will explain it to you.

See what I did there? This is harder than I thought. I'm telling you about my friend when what I said I wanted to do was come clean with you.

Okay. This is the truth. I'm just like my friend. When I said I never did the deed with anyone but my wife, that was a lie, because an orgasm is an orgasm. When I was a kid, I did everything I could to get my jollies as often as I could while still maintaining the pretense of virginity.

It's a beautiful thing, this capacity I have for self-justification. What it hides is that I was as lusty as the next guy. No more, maybe, but certainly no less. But the beauty of it was, I could be judgmental about the next guy because he was doing it, and I wasn't. You see how it works? I got sexual pleasure _and_ the reward of feeling better than someone else. What could be better than that?

You can try to let me off the hook if you want. You can say, "At least you weren't spreading sexually transmitted diseases. At least you weren't getting people pregnant."

Thank you. I appreciate your support. And you know what? What you're saying is technically accurate. …But, that doesn't make it true…

LIGHTS FADE.

discussion talk about it

Q: What stands out to you in Warren's monologue?

Q: Did he say anything that confused you? What?

Q: Did he say anything that makes you uncomfortable? Talk about that.

Q: Without embarrassing anyone, do you know anybody whose story is like Warren's? Talk about that.

Q: Have you ever heard the term _technical virginity_? What do you think it means?

How does Warren's story fit into your ideas about technical virginity?

Q: Warren doesn't think he's better than people who actually _did it_. What do you think about that?

Look at what Jesus says in Matthew 5:27-28. How does that relate to what we've been talking about?

Take My Breath Away

8

ARYN is a sadder-but-wiser high school senior. She's a plainspoken and faithful friend. Ayrn has Herpes. She's lucky that's all she has.

ARYN ADDRESSES THE AUDIENCE CONFIDENTLY.

ARYN

This'll take your breath away: 20 percent of Americans over the age of 11 have genital herpes.

Twenty percent is one in five.

You can stop looking around the room. It's not one out of <u>every</u> five—if you mean whenever five people are together one of them is infected. It's somewhat more complicated than that.

People with sexually transmitted diseases tend to cluster, so to speak. A few years back, there was this outbreak of gonorrhea in Colorado Springs—true story. Hundreds of people were infected, in all parts of the city. But half of them were from just four tiny neighborhoods. And half the infected people from those four neighborhoods hung out at the same six bars.

Got the picture? A huge—and hugely unexpected—epidemic was largely spread through the patrons of six bars in four small neighborhoods.

It gets better. Of the customers of those six bars—the ones who got the infection—fewer than 30 percent did the heavy lifting that turned the infection into a citywide epidemic.

GOOD SEX DRAMA

They did that by being gonorrhea evangelists. Not the kind who talk about it on the street corner...the kind who spread the love directly to their neighbors. That 30 percent, from six bars in four neighborhoods, was responsible for infecting from two to five people with their disease.

That's typical. A man in East St. Louis infected at least 30 women with HIV. I say women; that's not quite true. This guy took a special interest in 13- and 14-year-olds.

Same kind of thing happened in upstate New York. A guy infected at least 16 girlfriends with HIV.

And, of course, there was _Patient Zero_, the flight attendant who claimed to have sexual partners all over North America—hundreds of them, he said. Back in the 1980s, he was linked to at least 40 of the earliest cases of AIDS.

This is how sexually transmitted diseases spread. Most people who get infected are, more or less, victims. Don't get me wrong...they're victims of their own stupidity. They did something dumb and paid the price. Or they were arrogant enough to think, "Hey, this is me we're talking about. I'll be fine."

They're the ones—most of them—statistically, who get infected by the sexual storm troopers. They're the ones—I'm still talking about the hapless victims—they're the ones gullible enough to believe the liars who infect five or 15 or 40 others.

"He loves me. He really loves me."

They actually _participate_ in the lies.

"It's just this once."

"Okay, just once more. Then I'll be good."

"If it's not life-threatening, how bad can it be?"

"Are you kidding? I _know_ her. She doesn't have anything."

"Well we're not actually going to _do_ it. It's just, you know, oral."

Whatever the justification, I'm sure it makes sense at the time. Of course, that's the risk of making important decisions _at_ _the_ _time_.

Now you may be wondering how I know all this. You may be having a _Dawson's Creek_ moment, you know, "She _looks_ 17, but I'm pretty sure a 40-year-old put those words in her mouth."

Well, I'm a senior, as you know. So I have that going for me.

And my dad is an OB/GYN, so we have all this stuff—books and pamphlets and stuff—around the house. That's a female doctor for those of you with the other set of plumbing. And no, I don't mean my dad is a female doctor, so don't even bother going there—like I never heard that one before.

The other reason I know all this is because I did some research when I found out I'm one of the 20 percent of Americans with genital herpes. I'm one of the hapless, gullible victims.

That's the news that took _my_ breath away.

LIGHTS OUT.

discussion talk about it

Q: What grabbed you in Aryn's monologue?

Q: What do you know about herpes?

Q: What point was Aryn making with the gonorrhea story?

Q: What do you think of the term sexual storm troopers?

Q: Without naming names, do you know anybody who's a sexual storm trooper? Why might people act like that?

Q: Aryn talked about people who are "victims of their own stupidity." What do you think about that phrase? Are they?

Q: Are there do-overs for a person like Aryn? Talk about that.

If you need an explanation about do-overs, see page 5.

Q: Using the one-in-five ratio, how many people at your school could potentially infect someone with the herpes virus?

THE VOLUNTEER 9

FERNE is fortysomething and a little on the prissy side, though she means well.

GINNY is a volunteer youth worker. She's a reasonably cool middle-ager.

GINNY AND FERNE CHAT OVER COFFEE.

optional props...

HANGING OUT STUFF
2 coffee cups
coffee pot
table and 2 chairs

FERNE
You're exaggerating. How bad could it really be?

GINNY
Bad. It could be very bad. How long since you spent time around kids?

FERNE
I don't know. A while I guess. Still, I don't see what you're worried about.

GINNY
That's _why_ you don't see what I'm worried about. They're teenagers, Ferne. When they feel safe, they just say whatever they're thinking. They ask questions, very direct questions.

FERNE
So? That sounds refreshing.

GINNY
So, it's embarrassing. Refreshing, I don't know so much about.

FERNE
Oh come on, Ginny. Think back to your own youth.

GINNY
Nope. I was tricked. When I signed on to help with the youth group, I thought I was gonna bring cookies. I didn't know I would have a group of sophomore girls.

FERNE
I don't see the problem, Gin. You open the lesson, you read what it says, the girls pass notes and giggle, you close in prayer. Isn't that how it goes?

GINNY
You must be 150 years old.

FERNE
I don't think that was necessary. I'm just trying to help. You seem discouraged.

GINNY
I'm not discouraged, Ferne. I'm terrified. I'm overcome by waves of nausea. I'm paralyzed.

FERNE
You'll do fine. You're a very talented person.

GINNY
Don't pimp me, Ferne.

FERNE
Ginny! Don't what?

GINNY
See what I mean? I've been to, like, three meetings and my vocabulary is tweaked. Oh Lord, help me! I just said _like_…and _tweaked_!

FERNE
They talk like that? They say _pimp_?

GINNY

You wouldn't believe what they say. Especially if they think no one's listening.

FERNE

Well…it *is* a new century…and someone has to do it— I'm sure my time will come. I think you're overreacting.

GINNY

Then let me spell it out. For starters, Jules is in the group. She's not in *my* group but…just knowing she's in the room makes me nervous.

FERNE

For goodness sakes, why?

GINNY

Well think about it, Ferne. Would you want to look across the room and see your mother in the youth group?

FERNE

Not my mother, no. But you're nothing like my mother.

GINNY

She says she likes it. She says her friends think I'm cool.

FERNE

Well, there you have it! The young people think you're cool.

GINNY

We don't call them *young people,* Ferne, it's, it's…look, you weren't paying attention were you? The problem is these people ask questions. Nothing is off limits. They have no unexpressed thoughts…

FERNE

And…? I mean, for goodness sake, Ginny. You have a rare opportunity to influence these young minds.

GINNY

Oh, please! Do you have any idea how ridiculous that sounds? No wonder they think we're worthless.

FERNE

I don't think that was necessary. I'm trying to be upbeat.

GINNY

Just nod and smile then. You can't refer to them as *young minds*. They're people, okay?

FERNE

Why are you attacking me? Are you taking your medication?

GINNY

Ferne, you open your mouth, and I am amazed.

FERNE

Was that another shot? Because this hostility is very unattractive. Let me remind you, this is not about me.

GINNY

You're right. I'm sorry.

FERNE

Apology accepted.

GINNY

Thank you. Look, can I be straight with you?

FERNE

Can you be straight with me? Well, Ginny, that depends. Are you asking permission to be rude?

GINNY

Clearly, I don't need permission to be rude. Again, sorry.

FERNE

All right then. I believe you. Go ahead.

GINNY
Here's the thing: We're going to talk about sex next week, see…

FERNE DOESN'T REACT. GINNY CONTINUES.

…and, because we're going to talk about sex, that means six high school girls will ask me questions. And they'll expect honest answers. That's the kind of group it is. And over on the other side of the room, my daughter will be asking some other woman for honest answers…

FERNE
Oh…and you're worried about what that other woman will say.

GINNY
No. That other woman is the picture of balance and godly living. She's half my age and twice the woman I am. I couldn't be happier than to have her in Jules' life. What I'm worried about is what I'll say.

FERNE
Okay…you just keep being straight because I still don't follow.

GINNY
No, well, you wouldn't. That's why I want to try this out on you before it comes up in my group. Ferne, Darryl and I didn't make it to our wedding night.

FERNE
Sweetie, I was there at the wedding. Are you sure you're all right?

GINNY
We didn't make it to our wedding night, Ferne. We had sex before we were married.

FERNE

Oh…

GINNY

Oh?

FERNE

Well, what do you want me to say, Ginny? Oh, good for you? Oh, yay? You had a weak moment. You were both married before. You were both adults. It's a completely different situation than two teens. You see what I'm driving at?

GINNY

Ferne, put yourself in the place of a 16-year-old. Would you buy what you just said?

FERNE

I might if my youth leader told me to.

GINNY

Well thank you very much, Miss Compliance, because *I* certainly wouldn't, and I don't think you would, either. Who are you kidding?

FERNE

I only remain in this conversation because I care about you, Ginny. Your sharp tone would have driven away a lesser friend by now—I can tell you that.

GINNY

Again with the pimping. Wild horses couldn't drag you away now. You enjoy seeing me in this state.

FERNE

Maybe a little.

GINNY

Wipe that smirk off your face and tell me what I should do! I can't lie.

FERNE
I wouldn't rule that out just yet...

GINNY
(deadpan)
Very funny. Ha-ha. Stop! You're killing me.

FERNE
Perhaps we could fake your death. You could disappear and then resurface after this sex business is over.

GINNY
See? I knew you were enjoying this too much. I'm serious about this. Someone will ask me about my own sexual choices, and I'll have to bluff or tell the truth. Oh, who am I kidding? They'll catch me if I try to bluff; I know they will. They have little x-ray machines in their eyeballs. They'll see right through me. What's the oldest recorded case of mono? That puts people out of circulation for a while, doesn't it? I'll sit home and bake cookies until the sex thing is over. They'll send me cards and e-mail. It'll be great.

FERNE
What if you go to the leader—what's his name? Walter?

GINNY
Warren. Why don't I go to Warren and say what?

FERNE
Tell him you don't think it's a good idea to talk about these things in the context of the church. I'm sure there are other parents who would support you.

GINNY
It's so good I'm sitting down now.

FERNE
I think that's the wisest choice. Our young people need role models.

GINNY
Role models…

FERNE
People who have successfully…um…navigated their way through…the dangerous passages, let's say, of their, um, sexuality, you could say.

GINNY
I see.

FERNE
I knew you would. I think it's probably better to not go there at all—not at church, I mean. Because, isn't that what Sex Ed or Life Ed or whatever they call it nowadays—isn't that what that's for?

GINNY
They're only allowed to talk about <u>reproductive biology</u> in our school district.

FERNE
Well there you have it! Our elected officials have seen fit to limit our children's exposure to such things. I would think our pastoral leaders would follow suit, wouldn't you?

GINNY
You just keep talking, Ferne. You're making my decision easier and easier.

FERNE
There's that tone again. Listen, surely you agree the young people need role models. They need to learn about sex from people who—forgive me—they need to learn from people who haven't failed…sexually, I mean.

GINNY

Which is why you won't be volunteering to take my place.

FERNE

I don't think that was necessary.

GINNY

Well, in a perfect world, kids would learn about sex directly from Jesus.

FERNE

This is what I was trying to say. Let them learn it from Jesus.

GINNY

Yeah, well, it seems Jesus is unavailable to teach those weeks, Ferne. So, you know what? He sent me.

LIGHTS OUT.

discussion talk about it

Q: What stands out for you in this conversation between Ginny and Ferne?

Q: Who's comments—Ginny's or Ferne's—most reflect your interest in honest answers to honest questions? Put that on a scale of one to five.

Q: How would you react if you found out your youth leader didn't make it to his or her wedding night?

Q: If Ginny's group finds out, do you think the rest of the group will find out?

Will Jules find out? How would you react if you found out your own parents didn't make it?

Q: Do you agree with Ferne's statement that role models are people who haven't failed? Explain your thinking.

Q: Can a person like Ginny get do-overs? Talk about that.

If you need an explanation about do-overs, see page 5.

Q: What about Ferne? Do you think she needs do-overs? Why?

Q: Where do you imagine this story leads?

FREAKS 10

GINNY
is Jules' mom and a volunteer youth worker. She's a reasonably cool middle-ager.

JULES
is a smart, funny sophomore girl. She's uninhibited in ways that freak people out until they get to know her.

JULES IS FORCEFUL, HALF SERIOUS. GINNY IS CALM AND GOOD-HUMORED.

JULES
I don't see what the big deal is.

GINNY
And that's exactly what worries me, sweetie.

JULES
I'm not your sweetie right now, Mom.

GINNY
You're not?

JULES
Not right now. After. _Maybe_. Unless you're mean to me.

GINNY
I'm not trying to be mean, Jules.

JULES
I know. It just comes naturally.

GINNY
Your _friends_ think I'm cool.

JULES
They don't have to fight with you.

GINNY
Is that what this is? Are we fighting about this?

JULES
It depends on if you agree with me at the end.

GINNY
Well, we'll see how that goes.

JULES
Are you calm now?

GINNY
As opposed to…when?

JULES
When you told me there might be more than one way to look at, you know, that thing.

GINNY
Yes, I've come to my senses now. I'm certain you're right in every detail. Thank you for being patient with me.

JULES
You're welcome. So, what else would you like to talk about?

GINNY
How about if we talk about, you know, that thing?

JULES
Yeah, I suppose we could do that. Let me just state, for the record, one more time: I'm just kidding around, and you're the only one who's not perfectly clear about that. Okay?

GINNY
I understand that's what you believe. Will you humor me for a moment?

JULES
I suppose…as long as we're clear that you're out of your mind.

GINNY

Fair enough. Now you understand I'm not saying you're doing something wrong, right?

JULES

If you say so.

GINNY

I'm saying you're open to…misunderstanding.

JULES

I'm sorry, but it's hard for me to see the difference.

GINNY

Apparently, what *I'm* doing right now is open to misunderstanding.

JULES

This is different. I *know* what you mean.

GINNY

Tell me what I mean.

JULES

You mean I'm naive and stupid because I don't know how horny boys are. And can I just say how glad I am that I can say *horny* in front of you?

GINNY

Yes, you may say that, and, no, I am not saying you're naive *or* stupid. It gives me great pleasure to say you've misunderstood me completely.

JULES

Doh! All right, lemme try it one more time. You're saying I have to be mean to boys, or they'll think I'm easy, right?

GINNY

Uh…that's close, except for the part where you have to be mean to boys or they'll think you're easy. You wanna try again?

JULES
Okay, maybe once more. What you're saying is people dog me because… Okay, what are you saying?

GINNY
I'm *saying* you're not always careful around boys. I'm saying that sitting on their laps and hanging on their backs and giving full, pelvic hugs can be misconstrued.

JULES
By perverts.

GINNY
I don't think so, Jules. As you so delicately pointed out, boys are a horny lot.

JULES
Okay, can I just say I'm not completely comfortable when *you* say *horny*?

Look, I just think it's unfair that I have to watch what I do all the time. It's just frustrating.

GINNY
I know.

JULES
Do you? Because I'm not feeling a lot of support here.

GINNY
Jules, think about it: You weren't the first kid to be mad because you couldn't take off your shirt and play in the sprinkler.

JULES
Exactly. It's a double standard, and it makes me mad. I wanna take off my shirt and play in the sprinkler! They shouldn't be able to take that away from me.

GINNY
I'm sure there are boys who would agree with you on that.

JULES
They just want me to take off my shirt. Freaks. So how did you deal with this? Back in the day?

GINNY
Not all that well, really. I was pretty self-conscious—a lot more than you are, I think. I hit puberty early, and it kinda hit back, if you know what I mean.

JULES
I don't have the foggiest notion.

GINNY
Well, boys started to notice me, and girls started talking about me. I got in some sketchy situations with older guys, and they talked, which made the girls talk even more.

JULES
Okay, I've seen this. So…

GINNY
Your Aunt Vera caught wind of it and stepped in before things got out of hand. Of course I was furious. I was also relieved.

JULES
I see what you're doing here. You want me to think you're doing me a favor. Well, not so fast, Mom. I may have been born at night, but I wasn't born *last* night.

GINNY
Fine. Whatever…

JULES
Look at you! Talking like the young folk! Alright then, what happened next?

GINNY

What happened next is I got pretty crazy with food for a while—

JULES
(interrupting)
Like bulimia or something?

GINNY

More or less. I obsessed about getting fat, weighed myself two or three times a day, restricted my diet, tried pills for a while, tried chewing but not swallowing…

JULES

Mom! You were way ahead of your time! How could I not know this about you!

GINNY

It wasn't pretty. I've wanted to tell you about it. I just didn't know how to bring it up. It's not exactly dinner conversation.

JULES

You didn't throw up?

GINNY

Tried…couldn't do it.

JULES

I hear that. You know there are Web sites for this.

GINNY

I've heard.

JULES

I think it's stupid. No offense.

GINNY

No, you're right. Misguided, obsessed, stupid, sick…and _contingent_, Jules. Are you familiar with that?

JULES

Mom, of _course_. But tell me what _you_ mean by it. Just in case you're wrong.

GINNY

It means being dependent on something else in order to function. I was contingent on boys and fashion magazines for my self-worth. I covered my walls with pictures of smooth skin and zero body fat. And mirrors—so I could see how I was doing. It was crazy. It was weak.

JULES

Like how?

GINNY

Because it was a lie. Those pictures were doctored. They had perfect lighting, perfect makeup, perfect camera angles. They were altered to remove every blemish, every misplaced hair. Those girls didn't look like that in real life.

And because those magazines were about holding onto boys. As if that's why God put me on the planet—to be visually pleasing to men. As if my value as a human being were contingent on how I look to men. I believed it. I'm embarrassed by that, but it's true.

JULES

That's not how you raised me.

GINNY

I know. I've tried to tell you you're valuable just for showing up, just because God made you. I want you to be healthy. I don't care if you fit anybody's definition of beauty.

JULES

Are you saying I'm ugly?

GINNY

Yeah, pretty much.

JULES

Thanks for not letting me hear it on the playground for the first time... I think Grandma thinks I'm ugly.

GINNY

Grandma's a freak.

JULES

Mom! You called your mother a freak!

GINNY

Well she is. I love her, but she's a freak. I learned a lot of my craziness from her—but I'm feeling much better now. She's wrong, Jules. She's more interested in what you look like than what you truly are—and she's wrong... Are we clear about that?

JULES

Gee, no, Mom. What are you saying? I don't think I get it yet that you think your mother is a nut job.

GINNY

She's an appearance Nazi. Don't listen to her.

JULES

Well, I'm glad to see you've resolved all your hostility about this.

GINNY

Not even close, Jules. And you're caught in the middle. I'm sorry about that.

JULES

Just don't leave me alone with her. She makes cracks about my weight. I can take it when she goes off about my clothes. That's not me. But when she talks about my weight…

GINNY

I'll tell her to knock it off.

JULES

Look at you getting all fierce!

GINNY

I should have done it sooner. I should have protected you. Sorry.

JULES

It's okay. I'm all right.

GINNY

Yes, you are.

Now…about that sitting-on-laps-hanging-over-backs-full-pelvic-hug conversation. I'm not sure we got closure on that.

JULES

See, this was going so well. Now you have to bring up the past.

GINNY

You *wish* it were the past.

JULES

One of these days I'm going to get a therapist and tell her all about you.

GINNY

Bring it on. Look, I'll pay for college or therapy, pick one.

JULES
Hmm. Therapy's probably not a good place to meet boys and have hot monkey sex.

GINNY
You're a freak.

JULES
You're a freak.

LIGHTS OUT.

discussion talk about it

Q: What grabs you from this conversation between Jules and Ginny?

Q: What do you think about Ginny's concern that Jules isn't always careful around boys?

Q: What do you think of Jules point about the double standard?

Q: How believable is Ginny's early puberty story? Because...

Q: Talk about Ginny's idea of being dependent on boys and fashion magazines for self-worth.

Q: Have you seen examples of an older person putting undo pressure on a child or grandchild about appearance? What do you think about Jules' grandmother, the "appearance Nazi"?

Q: What do you think is Jules' responsibility around boys?

Q: Where do you think this story goes?

VOTE OF CONFIDENCE 11

GINNY is a reasonably cool middle-ager. She's Jules' mom, Darryl's wife, and a volunteer youth worker.

GINNY SIPS A CUP OF COFFEE AS SHE TALKS TO THE AUDIENCE.

optional props...
HANGING OUT STUFF
coffee cup
comfy chair

GINNY

The world seemed very different when I was young. I don't think people were different. But the world, I think, has changed.

I grew up during the tail end of what my father called the *sexual revolution*. It was before one in five Americans were infected with herpes, before chlamydia sterilized so many; before human papilloma virus put so many at risk of cervical cancer, before HIV killed so many. *Free love* is what some called it before we had any idea how foolish—how incredibly childish—that would sound later.

We didn't know what we didn't know. We got our ya-yas out—I got _my_ ya-yas out. And paid almost no price for it. If you don't count the attachment problems that doomed my first marriage—that circle like vultures over my marriage to Darryl.

I know I'm not supposed to say that…but there it is.

Darryl is utterly, heroically, committed to me. And I'm doing everything I can to make it work. But honestly? It'll be a God thing if this marriage survives my craziness. That's not something I would say to my daughter or husband. I think he knows; he's very insightful. But Jules is a simple soul. She's smarter than anything, but she doesn't yet know what's in people's hearts—what we're capable of doing to damage each other, not to mention ourselves. And it's not just from meanness, either.

So much of the damage comes from, just, _wishful thinking_. Free love…what a concept. I mean, who wouldn't like to believe in pleasure without strings? Okay, maybe you're smarter than me; maybe you wouldn't even think of sex without strings. Maybe connection is what you want most. I could believe that. It's where I am now.

That's not where I was as a girl. I was desperate to not become my mother, to not copy her hang-ups and fears. So I didn't. I grew up to be me—with all _my_ hang-ups and fears. What a joke! I was very mean to my mother. And very arrogant. I held her in such contempt. Not that she was perfect. Please. But she wasn't…she _isn't_ worse than me. She isn't even that different. We just learned the same craziness in different ways.

Now I look at Jules and wish it were possible to grow up without hang-ups and fears. It's not. I see that now.

That sounds hopeless, I know. But it isn't. I did things I wish I hadn't done, things I ought not to have done, things I regret, things I'd take back if I could—but I'm not hopeless.

Those are the very things that drive me to God…because it's _so_ clear I don't have what it takes to… just _live_. I no longer trust myself to do the right thing. I'm too self-centered, too insecure, too…well, you know.

I wasn't married when Jules was born. I know she's done the math, but we've never talked about it. We will, of course. If she doesn't bring it up soon, I will. I _think_ I will. There again, God will have to help me. The Bible talks somewhere about believers who worship by the Spirit of God, who glory in Christ, and put no confidence in the flesh. By that definition, I'm a true believer. If the Spirit doesn't arouse worship in me, I'm just incapable of getting outside myself. If Jesus doesn't create good in me, there's a better than even chance I'll behave badly. I just have no confidence in myself anymore.

But you know what? I'm okay with that now. I may be a lousy example of human goodness, but, as my friend says, "I'm not _NOT_ good enough to show people who I truly am, and how I truly need Jesus." Warren, the youth worker at my church, says that's the main qualification for youth workers: to point kids beyond themselves to the goodness of Jesus. _That_ I can do, believe me.

LIGHTS OUT.

discussion talk about it

Q: What grabs you from Ginny's monologue?

Q: Ginny thinks the free sex she grew up with wasn't free at all. What do you think about that?

Q: Ginny mentioned she didn't experience any physical consequences of her sexual behavior as a young woman. Did you notice she didn't include her unwed pregnancy as a physical consequence? Talk about her choice.

Q: Ginny says she escaped disease from her early sexual experiences, but she didn't escape relational problems. What do you think about that?

Ginny talked about the relational damage done by wishful thinking. What examples of wishful thinking have you seen around you (or maybe in your own mirror)?

Q: Some people feel cheated because the risk of infection makes sexual experimentation more dangerous than it was for their parents' generation. What's your response to that?

Q: If your parents knew what Ginny just told us, how do you think they'd feel about having her involved with this group?

How would you feel about having someone like Ginny involved in this group?

Q: Ginny refers to Philippians 3:3, a verse about true believers who worship by the Spirit of God, glory in Christ Jesus, and put no confidence in the flesh. Do you think a person has to fail like Ginny failed in order to understand that idea? Explain your thinking.

Q: What does our discussion suggest to you about the reality of do-overs for people who fail sexually?

If you need an explanation about do-overs, see page 5.

THE URGE 12

NIXON
is a quiet sophomore boy with a dark struggle.

WARREN
is the youth worker in charge. He's married to Sarah; his age doesn't matter. Warren is half comic, half prophet, and half Greek chorus. Warren has a thing or two to say about a thing or two.

WARREN ADDRESSES THE AUDIENCE; NIXON LOOKS DOWN AT HIS SHOES. THE TABLE—WITH THE PAPER AND ENVELOPES ON IT—AND THE CHAIRS ARE PLACED DOWNSTAGE.

> **optional props...**
> **HANGING OUT STUFF**
> table and 2 chairs
> about 200 letter-sized envelopes
> about 200 flat sheets of copy paper
> one small spiral notebook

WARREN
I could tell something was up. And I could tell Nixon was almost, *just about*, ready to talk about it. Almost. Just about.

WARREN ADDRESSES NIXON.

WARREN
So what's up?

NIXON
Not that much. What are you up to?

WARREN
Same old.

NIXON
That's cool.

WARREN STEPS TO THE TABLE; NIXON FOLLOWS.

WARREN
I hafta get this calendar in the mail. You wanna give me a hand?

GOOD SEX DRAMA

NIXON

I guess. What do I have to do?

WARREN

Just fold it like a letter.

NIXON LOOKS AT WARREN FOR MORE DETAIL. WARREN RESPONDS.

Oh, right. You don't do paper. Fold it in thirds so it fits in a number 10 envelope…that's one of these.

THEY BEGIN TO FOLD THE PAPER AS WARREN CONTINUES.

So what've you been doing?

NIXON

Not much. School. Poetry.

WARREN

You like poetry? I did not know that.

NIXON

Yeah. Kind of. I have this book.

WARREN

Yeah? I don't know many guys your age who like poetry. Who's it by?

NIXON

It's by me. Sometimes I just fool around with words and stuff. A little. You know.

WARREN

Yeah? I'd like to read that some time…if that's okay.

NIXON PRODUCES THE NOTEBOOK FROM HIS BACK POCKET AND HANDS IT OVER.

NIXON

Yeah. If you want.

WARREN
Oh. Okay, thanks. Cool.

WARREN ADDRESSES THE AUDIENCE.

I figured Nixon for the skull-and-lightning-bolt type, know what I mean? Pencil sketches of human skulls with rats crawling out the eye sockets—that kind of thing.

This is how stupid I am.

His notebook is half full of short verses. Not very skillful, most of it, but real. True.

NIXON RECITES TO THE AUDIENCE.

NIXON
Just shut the door now.
Go to your room
and shut the door now.
I don't have time now.
Come back when you
grow up.

WARREN ADDRESSES THE AUDIENCE.

WARREN
I think that about says it.

WARREN ADDRESSES NIXON.

So, Nixon, I appreciate you trusting me with your poems.

NIXON
Sure.

WARREN
How long you been writing?

NIXON
A while.

WARREN
When did you start?

NIXON
A while back.

WARREN
Uh huh. Tell me how you write. Do you have to be in the mood? Do you have a special place? Just tell me about your process.

NIXON
I don't know. I just write. What do you mean?

WARREN
I have no idea. I'm just interested.

NIXON
Okay. Thanks.

WARREN
Can you tell me about this one?

WARREN ADDRESSES THE AUDIENCE.

Observe the no-fly zone.
This is your only notice.

NIXON PICKS UP THE RECITATION.

NIXON
Do not test this sovereign nation's resolve.
Violators will be brought down
without warning.

WARREN
That's pretty serious. Were you angry?

NIXON
When I wrote that? No, not especially.

WARREN
Earlier, then?

NIXON
What do you mean?

WARREN
You were angry earlier—before you wrote this?

NIXON
I guess.

WARREN
Nixon, tell me to jump off if you want, but I had the feeling you wanted to talk about something. Did I get that wrong?

NIXON
No.

WARREN
No what? No, I got it wrong—or no, I didn't get it wrong? What's on your mind, bud?

NIXON
You didn't get it wrong. I want to talk about it. But it's kind of hard.

WARREN
Okay…

NIXON
Do you ever…like, feel the urge to do something you know is wrong?

WARREN

All the time. Everybody does. What's up? You struggling with something?

NIXON

It's hard to talk about.

WARREN

That's okay. Take your time. Is it something you're tempted to do every day?

NIXON

Not really. I think about it almost every day.

WARREN

Well, when are you tempted? Am I saying that right? You said something about the urge to do something you know is wrong. Is it, like, a temptation?

NIXON

I suppose. I don't know if there's a difference. I feel it…mainly on weekends. And summers, I guess.

WARREN

Nixon? I need some help here.

NIXON

That's mostly when I baby-sit.

WARREN

Oh. So, are you tempted to, like, steal stuff or what? What's the nature of this urge?

NIXON

This is hard. It's sick, I know it is. Sometimes I have the urge to, I don't know, _hold_ the children.

WARREN

Like, sexually?

NIXON

I don't think of it that way.

WARREN

How do you think of it?

NIXON

Romantic, I guess. That sounds wrong when I say it out loud. It is wrong, isn't it.

WARREN

There's nothing romantic about touching a child sexually, no.

NIXON

Yeah.

WARREN

So…have you…?

NIXON

No! No. But I keep thinking about it. I don't want to, but I keep thinking about it.

WARREN

Well, for starts, Nixon, do you really think you should be in the baby-sitting business? With this struggle going on and all?

NIXON

I don't know. I haven't done anything.

WARREN

Ah, well…let me put it to you straight: you should *not* be in the baby-sitting business. I know there's a logic that says, "If I stop baby-sitting, that means I have a problem," right?

NIXON

I guess.

WARREN
Well, Nixon, we're having this conversation because you know this urge is a problem. You have nothing to prove by putting yourself in that position over and over again.

NIXON
But I love children. And my families depend on me.

WARREN
And you don't know what to tell them.

NIXON
Yeah.

WARREN
Nixon, true story. Have you done anything that anyone on the planet would consider inappropriate in any way? Not in your mind but physically?

NIXON
With a child?

WARREN
To a child.

NIXON
No. I've had some dreams that seemed so real I wasn't sure when I woke up. But, no. I haven't done anything.

WARREN
Okay, then. Look, you don't have to tell them anything. You just go get a part-time job or take A.P. English or go out for the play.

NIXON
I can't act.

WARREN

Then join the stage crew. Run the lights or something. But you need to stop baby-sitting. *Right* *now*!

NIXON

Okay. You think that will do it?

WARREN

No. I think that will get you out of danger—out of *that* danger at least. I don't think it answers the question you're asking though.

Nixon, I don't claim to be an expert or anything, and I'm not saying I've talked to a lot of people, but the people I *have* talked to about this all say the same thing: when they were little, someone older touched them inappropriately. They *all* say that.

Is that true of you, Nixon? When you were little, did someone do to you what you feel the urge to do sometimes?

NIXON CONCENTRATES VERY HARD ON PLACING FOLDED CALENDARS INTO ENVELOPES.

WARREN

Nixon?

LIGHTS OUT.

discussion talk about it

Q: What grabbed you in this exchange between Warren and Nixon?

Q: Why do you think Nixon is so fuzzy about this?

Q: What do you think of Warren's advice to Nixon?

What would you add to what Warren said?

Q: Warren thinks a history of sexual abuse is widespread among people who're tempted to abuse others. What do you think about that?

Q: If you were Nixon's friend, what would you do?

Q: Where do you think this story leads?

One More Call

DARRYL is an assistant principal, and he's sick to death of sexual craziness at school. Darryl is the administrator you'd most likely go to in a pinch.

DARRYL SITS IN A DESK CHAIR. HE TALKS TO THE AUDIENCE.

DARRYL

I don't mind telling you. This is *not* why I got into education.

If I have to call the child protection officer one more time about a sexual abuse case...

Ah, who am I kidding? I'll make that call before the month is out. It's a sick fact of life around here.

Did you know that 70 percent of teenage pregnancies are fathered by men over 20? <u>Seventy</u> <u>percent</u>! It's ridiculous! We've got this stupid older-man-younger-woman thing going...this *Pretty Woman* thing.

I mean it's been like that forever. Some old geezer like Spencer Tracy or Richard Gere or Sean Connery gets turned into a sex object for the likes of a Kathryn Hepburn or Julia Roberts. It's a complete fantasy! People like that don't exist. But a girl can hope, right?

Some greaser comes along with a car and a part-time job and, okay, so he's not Denzel Washington, but he's not all pimply and awkward, either. He makes her feel like a woman and, of course, he wants her to *act* like a woman, right? No way! He wants her to act like a girl. He wants her to do whatever he says. He wants oral sex and vaginal sex and whatever kind of sex he can get, and he's not afraid to be demanding if that gets him what he wants

optional props...

HANGING OUT STUFF
desk
desk chair
telephone
tape dispenser, stapler, pen holder, etc.

better than being tender. Oh, and he wants to keep it a secret from her parents. Real mature. Of course, she's only too happy to oblige because _she's_ so mature.

Speaking of oral sex, if I have to tell one more parent I just pulled her seventh grade girl off some boy behind the gym…

Humph. That's another call I'll have to make before the month is out. And the call to the boy's parent is always a delight. Mainly it's denial, or it's barely disguised pride. "Not my boy! My boy sings in the choir! If it was my boy, some slut tricked him. Not my boy!" Makes me wanna puke.

I don't know what's worse. Some parents are okay with it. For their sons, I mean. I suspect they'd feel differently if it were their daughters. We depersonalize girls so much in this culture. If it's not _our_ daughter, then she's meat. I'm sick of it.

At the spring dance? We found a girl in the boys' room, down in the last stall, toxically drunk—and a parade of boys going in one after another, actually leaving their dates on the dance floor to go stand in line and have a go at this kid.

Lord, she was a mess. Drunk and covered with vomit—the floor smeared with it—and semen. And blood. It was awful. And not one boy came and told anybody what was going on. Not one. The maintenance guy went in to check the paper towels and realized something was up.

And I'll tell you what I thought was the bigger betrayal. There were girls who knew she was in there, who saw her go in there and knew she was too drunk to look after herself. They _knew!_ And none of them told anyone either. Was she meat to them, too?

The girl—I can't say her name, but it wouldn't be hard to figure out who she is—the girl survived the alcohol poisoning, but she didn't come back to school. When she woke up in the hospital and started to piece together what happened, they had to transfer her to a psychiatric facility. Which is where she stayed, I understand, until the insurance ran out. I don't know how that will end. Not well, I think.

It was part of the buzz the next Monday at school. Less on Tuesday, though our counselors were starting to see a lot of students. By the end of the week it was a non-event as far as I can tell. There were lawsuits and expulsions, and there won't be any school-sponsored dances next semester. But that lovely little girl—who lived her whole life on the edge of popularity—she just doesn't exist any more. And that doesn't work for me.

I really don't know if anyone learned anything.

That's not why I got into education; I can tell you that.

LIGHTS OUT.

discussion talk about it

Q: What grabbed you about Darryl's monologue?

Why do you think that stood out for you?

Q: Do you agree with him about the older-male-younger-female fantasy thing? Talk about that.

Q: Listen to this quote from Michael Gurian (*The Wonder of Boys*, Tarcher/Putnam, 1999, page 239):

> "Most adolescents spend one second learning the discipline of intimacy for every hundred hours they absorb distorted images of intimacy from media and other kids.
> "A movie like *Pretty Woman* is a wonderful case in point. Here is a very entertaining Hollywood film, which is purportedly about love. In fact it's only about the first stage of love—romance of the mating ritual. Once the couple has mated, the movie ends. It is like 99 percent of the movies, stories, and books we read. Love, in this unreal model, is too easy, not a discipline but a series of conversations and little tiffs that lead to sex and marriage.
> "To an adult who knows better, *Pretty Woman* is just good entertainment. To a boy, *Pretty Woman* teaches not discipline but fantasy."

What do you think about this quote?

Q: What do you think about Darryl's idea that we treat girls like meat?

Q: Will Darryl hang in there or look for a new line of work? Talk about which you think would be better.

Q: How about the girl at the spring dance—what do you think will happen to her?

What do you think it will take to stop that kind of thing from happening?

Promise Me: Late Night

14

[EPISODE 1]

BILLIE
is Meliss' mom. She's not stupid, she's just...naive.

MELISS
is a junior who's so busy with other people's business that she doesn't look at her own life very closely. She's good at misdirection and making mountains out of molehills.

IT'S LATE AT NIGHT, AND MELISS IS ON THE PHONE IN HER BEDROOM.

optional props...
HANGING OUT STUFF
phone
bed, blankets, and pillow
school books
clothes and other bedroom clutter
pajamas for Meliss
robe for Billie

MELISS

Because. You have to promise me you won't.

You have to promise me.

...Yes you do...Because he's not gonna change.

Oh you are so naive...No, no, *no*! Do *not* hang up on me!

Look. I'm not saying he won't ever change. I'm just saying you won't change him.

That *is* what this is about. You are *so* in denial, Toby! Yes, you are!

Right. If you don't give him what he wants, you think he'll still be your "friend"? You think he won't go find it somewhere else?

Not *yet*...Please! Of course, he will. He's...he has done it before.

No, it won't. Why? Why would it be different? You really think you're that special? You give him what he wants and see how special you feel.

GOOD SEX DRAMA

No...no that's not what I'm saying. You know that's not what I mean. You're the best. You know I love you. Just...

...Yes! I'm just saying you're not the first one who tried to rescue him, and I don't think you'll be the last.

BILLIE CALLS FROM OFFSTAGE.

BILLIE

Honey? Is that you?

MELISS

(whispering)
I gotta go. Yes. Meet me before school. Bye.

MELISS OPENS A BOOK AS BILLIE APPEARS IN THE DOORWAY, SLEEPY.

BILLIE

Are you still up?

MELISS

Hey, yeah. I'm almost done.

BILLIE

I don't think you're getting enough rest.

MELISS

Mom, I'm fine. I just have a lot of work. I'll catch up this weekend.

BILLIE

You have the wedding this weekend.

MELISS

Then I'll catch up next weekend. Please don't worry about me. I'm fine. You know how school is.

BILLIE

Is it school or the way you *do* school?

MELISS
It's school, Mom. Do we have to do this now? I'm trying to get to bed. I have to meet Toby before class.

BILLIE
Then you'd better finish and get that light out.

MELISS
Mo-om. I know-o. That's what I'm trying to do, but someone is in my room talking to me.

BILLIE
I just worry. I don't think you take very good care of yourself.

MELISS
Well, thanks for the vote of confidence, Mom. Look, I appreciate your concern, but I have to get through this myself.

BILLIE
A couple more years and I won't be able to look in on you like this.

MELISS
Exactly. And we'll probably both sleep better. Promise you won't worry about me? You have to promise.

BILLIE
Good night, Melissa.

MELISS SMILES SWEETLY AS BILLIE EXITS, THEN SURVEYS THE MESS AROUND HER.

MELISS
Well, so much for homework. Thanks a lot, Mom.

LIGHTS OUT.

discussion talk about it

Q: What grabs you from this scene?

Q: What do you think about Meliss?

Without embarrassing anyone, do you know anyone like her?

Q: What do you think is going on with her friend Toby?

Q: What do you think about Meliss' mom?

Q: Have you seen this kind of mother-daughter relationship before?

How healthy do you think this kind of relationship is?

Q: Where do you think this story is headed?

Promise Me: Let's Make a Deal

[EPISODE 2]

15

DARRYL
is an assistant principal who's sick to death of sexual craziness at school. Darryl is the administrator you'd most likely go to in a pinch.

MELISS
is a junior who's so busy with other people's business that she doesn't look at her own life very closely. She's good at misdirection and making mountains out of molehills.

MELISS IS IN DARRYL'S OFFICE.

MELISS
You understand this is not me, right?

DARRYL
I understand.

MELISS
So this is confidential?

DARRYL
Unless you convince me someone's life is in danger. Though you haven't said anything yet, so…

MELISS
This is just hard. I'm worried about my friend, and I know she won't help herself, so, if I can come up with something…you know?

DARRYL
Why don't you send your friend to see me? Or bring her?

MELISS
She won't come.

optional props…

HANGING OUT STUFF
desk
desk chair
telephone
tape dispenser, stapler, pen holder, etc.

GOOD SEX DRAMA

DARRYL

You suggested it already?

MELISS

There's no reason. I know she won't come.

DARRYL

And you know this because...

MELISS

Because it's how she is. She's dead set on doing things her own way. She never listens. Drives me crazy.

DARRYL

I know what you're saying. So, listen Meliss, if you already know she won't listen to me, what makes you think she'll listen to you?

MELISS

She trusts me. I mean I've been up with her almost every night this week. I call her every night to be sure everything is okay.

DARRYL

And, by <u>everything</u>, you mean...

MELISS

Okay, here's what's happening. My friend thinks she's in love with this, like, gangster. And she's all sure she can turn him back from being this, like, menace to society...to being, I don't know, student body president or something.

DARRYL

Student body president.

MELISS

Or whatever. I keep telling her he just wants to hook up, and she gets all snippy about it.

DARRYL

Because she believes she can save him.

MELISS

Exactly. But I know she can't because I've seen it before. He'll play her along as far as she'll go.

DARRYL

And you know this because…

MELISS

Like I said, I've seen it before. This kind of guy is only after one thing. He's a pooch.

DARRYL

A pooch.

MELISS

You know. A *pooch*.

DARRYL

Ah—a pooch.

MELISS

Exactly. So he'll take what he can get and move on.

DARRYL

Well, heaven knows I've seen boys like that in this school. What makes you think he's one of them?

MELISS

It doesn't take a genius, Mr. Potter. For starters he's all hip-hop and everything. And he dresses all urban and everything. I mean, come on. And they changed his name to *Repo*. Oops. Forget I said that. But do you wanna know *why* they changed his name to Repo?

DARRYL

Why did they change his name? And who is *they*?

MELISS

Well, his friends, his *boys*. And they changed his name because—he *claims*—he got all born again and stuff.

DARRYL

And stuff.

MELISS

I don't know. I don't hang out with people like that. They just claim he's a new man or something.

DARRYL

They...

MELISS

His *boys*.

DARRYL

Do they really call them that?

MELISS

I don't know. I don't hang out with people like that.

DARRYL

So, they changed his name to Repo because...he's...what? Acting different?

MELISS

I suppose. That's what they're saying.

DARRYL

His boys.

MELISS

Everyone!

DARRYL

Except you.

MELISS

Like I said, I've seen it before.

DARRYL

I see. Meliss, I know this isn't why you came in, but you've been late to first period a lot lately.

MELISS

I know, and I feel real bad about that. I'm having a little trouble getting started first thing in the morning.

DARRYL

This is a transportation problem? Because the bus is an option.

MELISS

The bus? Lord, no! I can't even get *here* on time. I'd never make the bus. That's, like, 6:30 or something.

DARRYL

Seriously, Meliss. This is a problem. Your name is on the referral list from Attendance this morning. That automatically generates a letter to your…what…your mother?

MELISS

Oh well that's perfect. That's just what I need.

DARRYL

Meaning…

MELISS

Oh, you know. Typical mother-daughter conflict.

DARRYL

Like what?

MELISS

She thinks I stay up too late, and I think she needs to give me more space...that kind of thing.

DARRYL

And is one of you more right than the other about that?

MELISS

I don't know, maybe. I could sure use more space—just kidding. I do stay up late; she's right about that. But you know how school is—listen to me, telling *you* how school is.

DARRYL

Yes, well... See, here's the thing, Meliss: if you can't make it to school because you're on the phone with friends...

MELISS SIGHS AND CROSSES HER ARMS.

...hold on, let me finish. You said you've been up late talking with your friend every night this week, right? So if you can't get to school on time because you're on the phone with friends who have problems, well that may be generous, but it also creates problems for you.

MELISS

It's worth it if I help them.

DARRYL

It might be worth it if you truly helped them, I'll grant you that. If I heard you right, you call your friend every night. Did I get that right? Or does she call you?

MELISS

I mainly call her. Because my mom doesn't like me talking on the phone late at night.

DARRYL

I see. And this solves that how?

MELISS
If I call out, the phone doesn't ring...

DARRYL
Ah. And if the phone doesn't ring, you're not talking late—

MELISS
Exactly.

DARRYL
—as far as she knows.

MELISS
Yes.

DARRYL
And you don't have a problem with that.

MELISS
If she would let me talk, there wouldn't be a problem.

DARRYL
Uh-huh. Because then you could help your friends with their problems *and* be at school on time.

Look. Everyone likes to feel needed. Me, you, everyone. No takeaway on that—

MELISS
That's not what this is.

DARRYL
Okay. I'll make a deal with you. You ask your friend to come see me...

MELISS LOOKS AT THE CEILING AND SHAKES HER HEAD.

...hold on—ask her to come see me with you this afternoon—

MELISS
(interrupting)

She won't come—

DARRYL

—to come see me with you this afternoon to sort out what kind of support she needs from you in her relationship with Mr. Reynolds. Come at the beginning of fifth period. I believe you have a class together at that time. I'll write you a pass right now.

MELISS

How do you know who I'm talking about?

DARRYL

That, Miss Perkins, is why they pay me the medium bucks, because I am just that smart.

MELISS

Hold on. So what's the deal?

DARRYL

The deal, Miss Perkins, is if she tells me she needs your support on a nightly basis, I'll speak with your mother about allowing Toby to call you each evening before she goes to bed.

Now I can't speak for your mother; she may overrule me on this, but I promise to make the case to the best of my ability. Does that seem fair?

MELISS

It does. You're a doll! I'll see if I can get her here at the beginning of fifth.

DARRYL

Very good. And Miss Perkins? Not so much with the "you're a doll" thing, okay? Bye-bye.

LIGHTS OUT.

discussion talk about it

Q: What stands out for you in this exchange between Meliss and Darryl?

Q: What do you think of Darryl and how he handled Meliss?

What do you think he's up to?

Q: Darryl seems to believe Meliss is looking for attention. What do you think about that?

What evidence do you see that supports your belief about that?

Q: Meliss believes Repo is a pooch. What do you think of her reasoning?

Q: Where do you think this story is going?

Promise Me: After the Fire

[EPISODE 3]

16

MELISS is a junior who's so busy with other people's business that she doesn't look at her own life very closely. She's good at misdirection and making mountains out of molehills.

TOBY is a junior girl who's honest but not always direct—until she's cornered; *then* she tells it straight.

MELISS AND TOBY TALK HEATEDLY.

MELISS
I can't believe he lied to me!

TOBY
He didn't lie to you, Meliss.

MELISS
Well, he set me up. He knew what you would say.

Why didn't you just *tell* me I was intruding? All you had to do was say something. I was only doing it to help.

TOBY
Meliss, I tried to tell you. Do you know you woke me up three times this week?

MELISS
I did not. You said you were studying.

TOBY
One time! The other three nights I was sound asleep when you called. My father was *not* pleased.

MELISS
Does he have a no-call rule too? Why didn't you tell me?

GOOD SEX DRAMA

TOBY

Meliss, *I* have a no-call rule! It was *11:30*!

MELISS

You don't have to get all snippy about this. I was just trying to help. What did you tell your father?

TOBY

I told him you're all in a crisis 'cuz you have a boyfriend problem.

MELISS

Me?!

TOBY

You appear to have a very big problem with my boyfriend.

MELISS

Very funny.

TOBY

Thank you. Thank you very much. And here's the thing, Meliss: I'm not going out with Repo.

MELISS

He has lunch with you every day!

TOBY

And Knox and Aryn and sometimes Jules.

MELISS

Yeah, what's up with that? That girl is strange.

TOBY

Well, Jules is a long story. She's also Mr. Potter's stepdaughter. And her mom, Ginny, is a volunteer in my youth group, which is also Knox's and Jules' group. And guess who else just joined? Repo.

MELISS

Reeeeally.

TOBY

Yes, really.

MELISS

See, I saw those other ones at the table, but I didn't know they were with you.

TOBY

Well, they were. They *are*. We're all just one happy little family.

MELISS

Is it true, then—about Repo?

TOBY

Depends on what *it* is. What did you hear?

MELISS

First, I heard he was under indictment or something. Then I heard he went underground to stay out of jail. I heard he said he met God or something and was taking sanctuary in the church. You really call Mr. Potter's wife *Ginny*?

TOBY

Uh, yeah. It's how she introduces herself. It's that kind of group.

MELISS

So is any of what I heard true?

TOBY

Not a word. His mom came to a divorce recovery thingy at the church, and there was a night when the kids were invited. So he came with her, and I guess he must have liked it because the next night he was at youth group. The rest, as they say…

MELISS
…Is history. So you're not going out.

TOBY
I'm sure I'd be the first to know. And you, no doubt, would be second.

MELISS
But you _would_ go out with him.

TOBY
It's not even a question, Meliss.

MELISS
It's not a question that he asked and you said no? Or it's not a question that _if_ he asked you would say yes? Because I see what's he's up to. He's pooching for virgins. That's what you all are, right? With your little pledge rings? I mean I am, too, but not for any weird, religious reasons. See? I _was_ right! He's, like, a wolf among sheep or whatever. Watch yourself. Everything I prophesized could happen, just like I said.

TOBY
Meliss…you are such a freak. Okay. First I have something to say about pledge rings, and then I have a _strong_ recommendation, okay?

Look, you may think the whole pledge ring thing is bogus—I mean it's just a ring, right? But there's more to it. They really work if you understand how to use them. Pledge rings are 100 percent effective—100 percent—if a girl will slip the ring off her finger and grip it very tightly between her knees.

MELISS
You are a sick, sick girl. I am way out of my depth with you. You need serious help.

TOBY

Thank you. Thank you very much. Look, my strong recommendation, Meliss—and I really mean this: get a life of your own! You have way too much time to yourself. Get out and meet some people. Come meet Repo. We have lunch together just about every day. Come meet Ginny for goodness sakes. I see her every Wednesday night. The woman is a hoot. I can hardly believe she's somebody's mother. Seriously. Get a life.

Okay? So, I have to go now. Remember that tip about the pledge ring.

LIGHTS OUT.

discussion talk about it

- **Q:** What grabs you in this exchange between Meliss and Toby?
- **Q:** What do you think of Toby?
- **Q:** Why is it so hard to get through to people like Meliss?
- **Q:** What do you suspect is going on with Repo?
- **Q:** Where do you think this story is leading?

REPO 17

REPO is a junior boy with a tough reputation. He's also a changed man, working to leave his old life behind.

REPO SPEAKS TO THE AUDIENCE.

REPO

Of course…sure. If I knew then what I know now, I would have done things different, you know? Of course.

There's lots of things I regret. The drugs, the sex. I wish I could take it back. I'll probably spend the rest of my life making amends for that. I don't know.

My biggest regret is the young ladies I hurt. I don't know if I knew I was hurting them exactly, but I sure knew I wasn't helping them at the time. I mean, I wasn't really even thinking about them. I was mostly thinking of myself, you know?

Okay, this may sound bad because there's no excuse for it, but…it's the way I was raised, you know? I would see my father around town, always with a different girl, always with his arm around her. He left when I was a little kid, so he wasn't a role model exactly, but I watched him. I saw him around town.

A lot of the older guys were that way. I knew what was going on. My mom had boyfriends who stayed over. I watched. I listened. Kids learn things from TV, too, you know?

I talked like the men I saw. I talked like the videos I watched, like the radio. I think about it now…it was very disrespectful. I would never call a young lady *bitch* or *ho* today. That's not right. I think I kinda knew that all along.

But it's what I did; it's how I talked.

And how I talked is how I started acting. I called young ladies *ho's*, and I started thinking of them as ho's. Then I treated them like ho's, you know? Or tried to. Many young ladies don't put up with that stuff. But others were too afraid or too weak or too beat down… I hate that I did that to daughters of God. I just hate it.

I'm trying to get that turned around. I know I can't take it back or make it go away but… Truly, I don't know what I can do, but I feel responsible for what I did. I'm trying to make it right.

They started calling me *Repo*. It's a stupid name, but I guess it's true. It's like I've been repossessed by God, you know? Like I was…I don't know. I was pretty tweaked. I'm no prize now, but I was really out there. I did damage to myself, and, like I said, I was very hard on young ladies. I'm asking God to make that right. I'll do what it takes, you know? I'll do what it takes.

LIGHTS OUT.

discussion talk about it

Q: What grabs you about Repo's monologue?

Q: Have you known people like Repo?

Q: Repo said the culture he grew up in taught him to treat women badly. What do you think about that?

Q: Repo believes his language affected his behavior. What do you think about that?

Q: It sounds like Repo found that some girls were victims and some weren't. What's your response to that?

Q: Are there do-overs for a guy like Repo? Talk about that.

What about the girls he misused? Talk about do-overs for them.

If you need an explanation about do-overs, see page 5.

18 OUT OF THE MOUTHS OF BABES

REPO is a junior boy with a tough reputation. He's also a changed man, working to leave his old life behind.

VICTOR is a man in his 20s who volunteers with the youth group. He's HIV-positive and making the best of the rest of his life.

REPO AND VICTOR TALK COMFORTABLY TOGETHER.

REPO
You wanna know what shocked me?

VICTOR
Sure, Repo. What shocked you?

REPO
The amount of sex in the youth group.

VICTOR
Oh. Well, maybe that is shocking. Tell me more.

REPO
I'm new to this, you know? I expected things to be a lot different, you know?

VICTOR
Different from what?

REPO
From before. Different from my old life. I didn't expect this level of sexual activity, you know?

VICTOR
Well, you'd think.

REPO

Yeah…I would. Some of it is, you know, more or less harmless, I guess. That girl, Jules? Before she knew my name even, she sits on my lap. "You don't mind if I sit here, do you?" she says.

VICTOR

Ah, Jules. Well that's easy to explain. Jules is crazy. They're gonna lock her up in just about a minute.

REPO

Make a joke of it, but the wrong dude could make her a very sad girl. That's all I'm saying.

VICTOR

Hmm… that's a fair statement.

REPO

Anyways, Jules isn't who I'm worried about. She's just a little out there. Most of the guys here are scared of her.

What surprised me when I came here, and what worries me now, is this, like, electric current of sex that runs through the group. You know, people pairing off at camp and stuff. I mean, do you know what goes on in the back of the van?

VICTOR

I know it's loud.

REPO

That's the ones sitting <u>on</u> the back seats. The ones laying on the floor aren't saying much.

VICTOR

Oh. And is there a lot of that?

REPO

Alls I can say is if a trip takes more than a couple hours, a coupla people end up on the floor.

VICTOR

Why doesn't somebody just say, "Get off the floor, you freaks!"?

REPO

I don't know. Because they get away with it, maybe. Because so many of them have done it, maybe. There's, like, a code of silence. People look the other way.

VICTOR

It's part of the group culture—is that what you're saying?

REPO

They grew up doing it, if that's what you mean. Camp is even worse.

VICTOR

Do I wanna know this?

REPO

I think somebody better know it.

VICTOR

Why me? Why not Warren? He's in charge.

REPO

I don't know Warren. Like you say, he's in charge. Maybe he sends a signal that it's okay. I don't know what I think about him.

VICTOR

No, he's…he'd be very sad to hear what you're saying.

So tell me about camp.

REPO

I never was at a camp before, you know? So I was a little nervous and all.

Sure enough, this dude from the group—I didn't know him yet—he has this girl with him, and we're all in the back of the van, and pretty soon they slip down onto the floor. I mean, we're barely out of town. And I'm thinking, "Whoa. This ain't right." And I figure they'll get busted, but they don't.

So we get to camp, and they're all yawning and everything and getting everything tucked in and all, and I'm thinking, "This is whacked!"

So at dinner, I hear the rules and all. You know, "No boys in girls rooms and no girls in boys rooms. No taking other people's stuff." To be honest? All things I thought should go without saying at a youth group camp, you know?

VICTOR

Well, you'd think.

REPO

I would. I did. Now…not so much. What the rules didn't cover was how big that place was and how many empty rooms there were. I'm surprised nobody got pregnant.

And that just doesn't seem right to me. I think this should be a place where you don't have people taking advantage of your weaknesses, you know?

VICTOR

No one should ever take advantage here.

REPO

This is what I'm saying. Look, I gotta be honest with you. I slipped a few times when I first came. It took me by surprise. Maybe it shouldn't have, but it did. I'm embarrassed about that. Anyways, I did what I could to make it right with those girls. I don't know if they understood where I was coming from, but I tried to do the right thing.

And that dude I was telling you about: the one who was on the floor with his girl? Well I know him now. I busted his chops about that sh—sorry—I busted him about his inappropriate behavior, and you know what he did? He cried. Not like a girl or anything; he just filled up with tears and said, "Man? I never thought you'd be the one to hold me accountable for my actions." He said I was absolutely right, and he was sorry for being such a di—such a bad example—sorry. Anyways, we're, like, keeping each other accountable now.

VICTOR

That's amazing, Repo. Out of the mouths of babes…

REPO

Is that Christianese? I don't speak that too good yet.

VICTOR

Sometimes people trick themselves into believing actions don't matter as much as words—that what they *say* they believe is more important than how they behave.

REPO

That's what that means? Out of the mouths of babes? That surprises me. I woulda thought it meant something like, "It don't take a sanitation worker to recognize the smell of…" Oops, sorry. I can't finish that.

VICTOR

Yeah. That too, Repo.

LIGHTS OUT.

discussion talk about it

Q: What grabs you in this dialogue between Repo and Victor?

Q: What do you think of Repo's story?

Do you think Repo should expect the youth group kids to behave differently than kids outside of youth group? What would you tell him?

Q: Could that kind of thing happen in our group? Talk about that.

Without embarrassing anyone, how sexually charged do you think our group is?

Q: What do you think Repo and Victor should tell Warren, the group leader?

What do you think Warren should say—or not say—to the group?

Q: What do you think we can do to make our group safer than it is today?

ON A POSITIVE NOTE

19

VICTOR is a man in his 20s who volunteers with the youth group. He's HIV-positive and making the best of the rest of his life.

VICTOR ADDRESSES THE AUDIENCE.

VICTOR

People get weird when they find out. Which is mainly why I don't bring it up. I'm not a poster boy…you know? Of course, Warren knows. Nobody's hiding anything. It just doesn't come up very often.

When it does come up, people assume I'm dying. Which, I am. But not any time soon. My immune system is good, all things considered, and I'm taking care of myself, so…

Some people wonder if they can catch it from me—from casual contact, you know, shaking hands or playing basketball. I know a guy who was actually kicked out of his church because his wife and baby were infected. They got the virus from a blood transfusion. It was still early in the epidemic. People just didn't know. They were afraid to have the baby in the nursery. It was very sad. And unnecessary.

The virus is impossible to kick so far, but it's also fairly tough to catch. It spreads through blood or semen or vaginal secretions but only if it enters the second person's blood stream. HIV is fragile; sweat or tears don't transport it very well. I mean, if the van crashed, and I bled into your open wound, you could get it from me. I don't mean to be rude but, if that bothers you, ride in the other van, you know?

That said, *I* didn't get the virus from a transfusion. I got it from sex. Homosexual sex. Which was stupid because, by then, we knew how to prevent the spread of HIV. It wasn't just stupid. It was flagrant. It was…well? I guess it was a death wish.

…I don't know, that may sound crazy to you. So let me ask a question.

Do you have any idea what it's like to grow up as a boy who's attracted to boys? Probably not. So you probably wouldn't know what it's like to be that boy in a youth group.

Lemme just tell you that Christian people—do you know what I'm saying?—_Christian_ people said the most amazingly mean-spirited, hurtful things to me. Not about me specifically, since they didn't know about me, but, just, generally. I guess they thought it was funny, a lot of it. But not the fun that folks have with people they like. More the kind of fun people have at the expense of people they despise. Like whites who hate blacks and blacks who hate Asians and men who hate women. _That's_ how people in my youth group made fun of people like me.

I suppose they thought it was harmless because they didn't imagine there were people like me in the room. I mean, it's widely known that people like me have no interest in God, right? It's also widely known that God has no interest in people like me. I'm told that's in the Bible if you just read between the lines.

Well…I did care about God, and I was in the room, so…

The leaders said if we ever had any problems—any problems at all—we could always come to them. Always. And we did, a lot of us. *I* even did. When my parents split up, I don't know how I would have made it…

But I never talked about sexuality. Ever. In that atmosphere, why would I think my questions would be taken seriously? Not my *ideas*—I didn't have any ideas yet—my *questions*. I'm not a genius, but I mean, how often do you have to hear, "Dude! It's Adam and *Eve*, not Adam and *Steve*!"? I got that the joke was no joke.

So I lived through my youth group years in silence. I didn't laugh at the jokes, but I certainly never said, "Hey, that's me you're talking about!" And I never said, "Hey, you're talking about my friends!" because I had no friends. Acquaintances only. Limit exposure, limit pain. Simple risk management.

My college years are an embarrassing cliché. I watched openly gay students from a safe distance, stumbled across a gay bar near campus, put on a filmy shirt, went there, and nursed a diet ginger ale until some guy walked up and asked if I was gay. "How did you *know*? Oh my gosh!"

And that was that. I took a three and half year thrill ride. Acquaintances only. No attachments. Limit exposure, limit pain. Right?

I suppose it could have been worse. I could've been putting women at risk of disease and pregnancy like some of my friends from high school. Relax: I know that's not worse. I also know it's not better, you know?

You're gonna think this is strange, probably, but my last week of college I decided to treat myself to a blood test. It was like saying, "Okay, I'm grown up now." I guess I thought I would enter responsible adulthood with a freshly minted college diploma and a clean bill of health.

As you know, that's not how the blood test turned out.

After I freaked out for a month or so, I figured I'd better tell my parents everything because, sooner or later, I would start getting really sick, right? I assumed it would be sooner rather than later. They took the news very badly. It's, what—over five years now? And we're still walking on eggshells. I don't know how that will turn out.

Once I stopped freaking out, I started reading everything I could find—medical and moral. I got into a support group of infected people, came back to church, got in a Bible study—which is where I met Warren and Sarah a couple of years ago. We're pretty close.

About two months ago, Warren asked if I'd help with the youth group. I said, "You don't know what you're asking," and he said, "Yeah, I do. You're about the safest person I know right now."

He's right. I'm pretty much _asexual_ at this point. I'm not interested in girls—though some people say, "Be patient, you will be." I don't know…

For the record, I was never attracted to younger boys—I'm not a pedophile. As for guys my age…it's complicated but not impossible. The fruit of the Spirit is—do you remember?—_self-control_.

Some people say if I'd been free to date boys in high school that maybe I wouldn't have engaged in high-risk behavior later. I have no way of evaluating that. I knew girls in high school who caught and spread sexually transmitted diseases. And that certainly wasn't for lack of information or access to multicolored condoms, so… If I could have dated boys, it's possible I would have just gotten an earlier start in high-risk behavior.

"That's because the whole society is repressed," some people say. "If sex weren't considered dirty, we could eliminate sexually transmitted diseases." Okay, so look: now that I know I'm dying, I've entered a no-nonsense phase in my life. So I have to tell you straight up, I have no idea what that sexual repression argument is all about. Sex has been an abundantly available—if mainly scary—fact our entire lives, you know? We've talked it just about to death. We've made our choices, pro and con, and learned to laugh at the threat. I live in the world where movies show boys copulating with fruit pies, what world are you living in? You know?

Some people say I was born gay. They say homosexuality is a biological fact of my life, like the color of my hair and eyes. They say it with conviction; it's an article of faith for them. I have no way of knowing. The human genome has been completely mapped and, as of today, there's no evidence of a "gay gene." Who knows what tomorrow will bring? In any case, I'm not sure the discovery of a gay gene would get me off the hook. If an alcoholic gene is discovered and I have it, I'm still responsible for whatever I do under the influence. It could help explain some things maybe, but it wouldn't solve anything—for me at least.

Some people say I _chose_ to be gay. If so—and I've thought a lot about this—I don't remember making that choice. And I can't recall any series of small decisions that add up to a big choice to be attracted to men, either. As a child I didn't think much about it. When I entered puberty the attraction took on a sexual dimension. What else is new?

Some people say I'm sexually confused because I was sexually abused. I _am_ confused, I can tell you that. I don't think I know anyone who isn't. And I can confirm that I was molested repeatedly by a friend of my older sister. Was that the key factor in my sexual development? I don't know. And, for the record, neither do you—one way or the other.

Some people say my parents did this to me. The weak-father-strong-mother thing. Or is it the emotionally-abusive-father-mother-as-victim thing? Neither, actually. We were pretty ordinary from everything I can see. But how would I know? They're the only parents I ever had.

The people who say I chose homosexual attraction say I can <u>unchoose</u> it. I don't know about that. My night dreams are generally homosexual. I don't know if that's because, at the deepest level, I'm homosexual or because all my sexual experiences were homosexual. And I don't know how to find out. I wish I did.

There's a lot I don't know. You noticed that.

Here's what I <u>do</u> know: I love God because I know God loves me with all his heart. I don't have to read between the lines to find that in the Bible. I've given up the belief that I can get God to love me any more than he already does. And I'm trying to give up the fear that when I screw up God loves me less. I'm trying to trust God every day.

Meanwhile, I've chosen a life of celibacy—that means I'm not having sex with anyone. I just don't know how to satisfy my sexual desires without hurting people, so... I mean, there's already enough hurt, you know?

So there's no sex, but really for the first time, I'm letting people in my life. Warren, Sarah, some other folks you wouldn't know... And I asked my dad to lunch this week. I told the folks what I did, but I never really let them in on who I am. I figure I'll start with my dad and see how that goes.

It's a page turn. Limit exposure, limit pain? That really didn't work that well for me, so...here I am—love me or hate me.

But please love me.

LIGHTS OUT.

discussion talk about it

Q: What grabs you in Victor's monologue?

Q: Did he say anything you haven't thought about before?

Did he say anything that bothers you?

Q: Does it surprise you that Victor heard lots of mean talk in his youth group? Talk about that.

Q: Victor doesn't know if he has homosexual dreams because he's homosexual or because his sexual experiences were all homosexual. What do you think?

Q: What do you think about Victor's choice to be celibate?

Q: Some people say Victor was born homosexual, others say he chose homosexuality. Some say sexual abuse led to sexual confusion; others say it's his parents' fault. Victor says he doesn't know and neither do you. What do you think about that?

Q: What he does claim to know is that God loves him with all his heart. Some people would disagree with that. What do you think—and why?

Q: Knowing what you know about Victor, would he be welcome in this group? Talk about that.

Q: How do you think Victor's story plays out?

NOT THAT BIG A THING 20

ARYN is a sadder-but-wiser high school senior. She's a plainspoken and faithful friend. Ayrn has Herpes. She's lucky that's all she has.

CARYN is a bright, articulate junior, but she has a blind spot. She's foolishly trying to downplay the impact sexual misconduct has on her. It's not working.

ARYN AND CARYN TALK HEATEDLY.

ARYN
Well *sorry*. What would *you* call it?

CARYN
Why do I have to call it anything?

ARYN
You don't have to call it *anything*. I'm just saying you have to deal with it. It's not like it was an accident.

CARYN
I don't want to be a victim. It happened. Move on.

ARYN
Well, how's that working out for you, Caryn?

CARYN
Why are you buggin' me about this? Can we just change the subject?

ARYN
Absolutely. What do you want to talk about? Eating disorders? Substance abuse?

CARYN

You wear me out.

ARYN

What can I tell you? It's a character flaw.

CARYN

Look, I know people react badly to this kind of thing. I just think, with what I know, I can work through it...I don't know...more *smoothly* than other people. Don't worry about me falling apart. I won't do that.

ARYN

No, of course you won't. What you'll do is shut down. What you'll do is stuff your feelings, and, if they're too intense to stuff, you'll numb them somehow. Any of this sound familiar?

CARYN

No. Just leave me alone!

ARYN

Yeah, that'll happen.

CARYN

What is your *problem*? Get outta my head! Look, I'm in denial, okay? Is that what you want me to say? Isn't that the first stage? I can't believe it happened to me? Is that what you wanna hear? You want me to admit I'm...*typical*? Fine.

ARYN

Caryn, you are so *not* typical. You're the strongest person I know. I've seen you shut down an aggressive guy with one look. I've watched you stand up for people who can't stand up for themselves. You're smart, and you'll run the planet some day.

Which is why I won't accept that you're stuck. You *know* what to do. Why are you, of all people, stuck?

CARYN

Aryn, it's just so…_humiliating_. And upsetting. If it can happen to me, it can happen to anyone.

ARYN

It is happening—all the time. You can make it stop.

CARYN

He had no right.

ARYN

Absolutely no right.

CARYN

And he knows it.

ARYN

He can't believe he got away with it.

CARYN

He didn't get away with anything!

ARYN

He thinks he did.

CARYN

He won't even look at me!

ARYN

He won't look you in the eye. That doesn't mean he isn't looking.

CARYN

I'll smack him.

ARYN

Will you?

CARYN LOOKS AT ARYN, THEN LOOKS AWAY. ARYN CONTINUES.

ARYN

This is what I don't understand.

CARYN

I don't want everybody to know. I already feel sleazy.

ARYN

You didn't do anything.

CARYN

I feel sleazy.

ARYN

You know what? Everybody doesn't have to know.

CARYN

They will. You know they will.

ARYN

We'll tell his mother.

CARYN

What?

ARYN

No, listen! Boys get away with this kind of thing because no one tells their mothers.

CARYN

You're insane. I'm not doing that.

ARYN

We'll take Ginny with us. She's a grown-up. She probably knows his mother. Ginny will believe you; you know she will. And his mother will believe Ginny.

CARYN

I don't think so…

ARYN

It'll work. We'll tell his mommy and let her take care of it.

CARYN

You're nuts.

ARYN

It'll work. If Ginny's there, it'll work; you know it will.

CARYN

It'll be embarrassing.

ARYN

For *him*. She's a woman. She knows what boys are capable of. She probably knows she raised a little pervert.

I promise you this: he'll never tell a soul. I mean picture it. He's in the locker room with the guys. What's he gonna say—

ARYN DOES MOCK BOY VOICES AS SHE CONTINUES.

ARYN

"Hey, brah, my mom busted me. Yeah, I showed my pee-pee to this chick at church camp."

CARYN

Eeeeeuuu!

ARYN

"Yeah, it was cool. But then she told my mom."

"Whoa, *dude*."

"Yeah, I *know*."

CARYN

Shut *up*!

ARYN SHIFTS TO ADULT FEMALE VOICES NOW.

ARYN

"Ms. Fletcher, I understand your son exposed himself to a young woman at church camp. You must be so proud."

"Oh, Ginny, you know: It's not that big a thing."

CARYN AND ARYN

Aahhh!

CARYN

This is wrong on so many levels!

ARYN

What can I tell you? I'm an evil genius. You in?

CARYN

Let's call Ginny.

LIGHTS OUT.

discussion — talk about it

- **Q:** What grabs you from this scene between Aryn and Caryn?
- **Q:** Where did you think the story was going at first?
- **Q:** What do you think about Caryn's reaction?

    What do you think about Aryn's plan?

- **Q:** Some people minimize genital exposure with a boys-will-be-boys attitude. They agree it's rude, but they wouldn't call it wrong. What do you think about that?
- **Q:** If you know anyone who's been visually assaulted by a flasher, talk about how you think that affected her or him.
- **Q:** What do you think possesses a guy to expose himself?

    Do you think it's more sexual or more aggressive? Talk about that.

    How do you think that applies to other forms of sexualized harassment?

- **Q:** Where do you think this story leads?

W+S : LAMENT

21

[EPISODE 1]

SARAH
is a bright woman who volunteers with the youth group. She's married to Warren, the youth worker; her age doesn't matter.

WARREN
is the youth worker in charge. He's married to Sarah; his age doesn't matter. Warren is half comic, half prophet, and half Greek chorus. Warren has a thing or two to say about a thing or two.

optional props...
HANGING OUT STUFF
book
2 comfy chairs

WARREN ENTERS, LOOKING LIKE HE'S BEEN MUGGED. SARAH LOOKS UP FROM READING A BOOK.

SARAH
Warren? What are you doing home?

WARREN
Hey, I kind of live here.

SARAH
What's wrong, Warren?

WARREN SITS DOWN HEAVILY.

WARREN
Jonathan's been arrested.

SARAH
Oh no! What happened? Is Terese okay?

WARREN
He was…in an *inappropriate relationship* with a 15-year-old.

SARAH
Who told you this? Are you sure?

WARREN
There was a posting on my discussion board.

GOOD SEX DRAMA

SARAH
(dismissive)
Well, if it's on the Internet…

WARREN
It's true. I spoke with Terese. Please don't be short with me.

SARAH
I'm sorry. Is she okay?

WARREN
Devastated. Confused. Angry.

SARAH
How are *you*?

WARREN
Well. He's my mentor, you know? So…

SARAH
I am so sorry…

WARREN
Yeah, well, it's one of those things I guess.

SARAH
No offense but…is that the story you're going with? "It's one of those things"?

WARREN
It's the only story I have right now.

SARAH
What are you gonna do about the retreat?

WARREN
Shoot, I don't know. I have to come up with another speaker, don't I?

SARAH

Looks like...

WARREN

Well, that should be easy enough. Now that I've lost my mentor, I just have to find someone I can trust, right? How hard can that be?

SARAH

People screw up. That doesn't disqualify everyone.

WARREN

Doesn't it? I mean...if it can happen to Jonathan...

SARAH

I don't think it _happened_ to Jonathan.

WARREN

Exactly. And he's the best. He was the best. He _appeared_ to be the best...

See? Now I have no language to talk about him. I don't know who he is. Apparently, I never did. How can that happen? How can a person be so _not_ what he's supposed to be when he _appears_ to be exactly right? Exactly right.

I...I don't know if I have what it takes anymore.

SARAH

You haven't lost it, Warren.

WARREN

No. I mean...I don't think I ever had it. I thought I did. Now...

SARAH

You're tired.

WARREN

I'm not just tired. I'm afraid.

SARAH

I know.

WARREN

I'm not better than him.

SARAH

I know.

WARREN

Is it time to get a real job?

SARAH

What do you think?

WARREN

Maybe this is a warning shot.

SARAH

I don't know, Warren. Maybe it's just a cautionary tale. Maybe you were right. Maybe it's just one of those things that happens, only this time it happens to be someone we know.

WARREN

…We thought we knew.

SARAH

Someone we thought we knew. Maybe—when we get the whole story—maybe we'll find out we did know him.

WARREN

It'll never be over, Sarah. He has children. He has—his *identity* is tied up in ministry. He writes books and speaks at conferences. He's not just gonna go get a job at Starbucks and disappear.

SARAH
Or maybe he will. Maybe he'll get a regular job and stay home nights with Terese and the kids and put things back together.

WARREN
You think she'll take him back?

SARAH
I don't know.

WARREN
Would you?

SARAH
I…can't imagine what they're going through. I'd like to think I could forgive you if you did something like that.

WARREN
After you turned me into a eunuch.

SARAH
Yeah.

WARREN
I'd like to think I'd never put you in that spot—not in a million years. But, honestly? My mentor just crashed and burned. What if he taught me something that…you know…something that could put me in the wrong place at the wrong time with a 15-year-old? I mean…if it could happen to Jonathan…

AFTER A MOMENT SARAH, REACHES OUT TO HUG WARREN. HE HOLDS HER TIGHT AS THE LIGHTS GO TO BLACK.

discussion talk about it

Q: What grabbed you in this scene between Warren and Sarah?

Q: How do you think Warren feels?

Have you ever felt that way? Talk about that.

Q: How do you think Sarah feels?

Have you ever felt that way? Talk about that.

Q: You'll have to project even farther on this: how do you imagine Jonathan feels?

What do you think he should do?

Q: How about Jonathan's wife, Terese? How do you think she feels?

What do you think she should do?

Q: Their children are in grade school and middle school. How do you think they feel?

What do you think is in their future?

Q: How do you think the 15-year-old whom Jonathan was involved with feels?

What do you think lies ahead?

Q: How does the idea of do-overs play into this story?

If you need an explanation about do-overs, see page 5.

Q: What do you think Warren should say about Jonathan not showing up to speak at the retreat?

Some people believe, once the facts are established, we should speak plainly about the failure of Christian leaders. Others believe that undermines the gospel. What do you believe?

Q: How do you think this will affect the youth group where Warren and Sarah work?

Q: Take a few minutes and write two endings to this story: one happy, one sad. (Do this individually or in small groups.)

Which outcome seems more likely to you? Because…

W+S: Girl Talk

[EPISODE 2]

22

SARAH is a bright woman who volunteers with the youth group. She's married to Warren, the youth worker; her age doesn't matter.

SARAH TALKS TO THE AUDIENCE AS IF TO A FRIEND.

SARAH

Honestly? I worry about him—big time. He works insane hours for low pay at a job he loves so much he can't see straight. If I didn't work, he couldn't work; not this way. We couldn't afford it.

I don't begrudge him that. We both believe he's called to do this. At least for now. If we had a baby, that might change things. I don't know.

It's not the money that worries me. I think it's the stress. He puts out so much and comes home so exhausted so much of the time. Sometimes I think the stuff at home is more than he can handle. I know that's silly. Everyone has the stuff at home: the bills, the laundry, the piddly details that keep things going.

He always seems behind in those things. He always seems behind in everything. He's maybe not the most organized human being I know. I don't know. He's a big boy; when he gets tired of being behind all the time, he'll get his act together.

Meanwhile, we'll cope. I think what worries me is…his work is challenging and affirming to him in a way our marriage isn't. I don't mean things are bad, because they're not; things are good. But life at home includes more…duty, I guess, and less applause.

I love talking with Warren, but I never gave him a Standing O…you know what I mean? I think he feels like he's changing kids' lives at work, but…not so much at home. Home is where there's always not quite enough to go around, and there's no janitor to clean up and fix the plumbing, and there's no one hanging on every word he says.

Don't get me wrong. I'm not saying ministry is a day at the zoo. People are critical, kids screw around, the hours are brutal…I guess I already covered that. It's just, when he's working, there's always someone who needs him unspeakably and someone who tells him he's a lifesaver, and someone else who looks at him like he's Jesus…and that makes me nervous.

I have no question about his commitment to me, no question about his love. Maybe sometimes I worry about his endurance. The youth group is swarming with these little 16-year-old hardbodies who adore him beyond words. They tell him their problems and confess their sins. They feel so safe with him that, sometimes, they're not careful how they sit. They're not aware when they bend over and he can see all the way to China. They're not careful how they touch him…

I've watched boys' eyes roll back in their heads when they see how girls touch Warren. They love to hug him, love to rub his shoulders, want to sit on his lap, and…honestly… I'm glad it's him and not some other guys I know who _really_ wouldn't be able to deal.

That's not entirely true. I wish it weren't him, either.

See, I feel bad even saying this stuff. I love it that those girls feel safe with my husband. I know there are so few places they can go and not be hit on by lecherous men. I wouldn't want to take that away. _I_ had a youth worker I felt safe with once upon a time.

But I find myself wondering: was I careful enough around him? Did I respect his personal space? Sometimes I wonder: did we drive him crazy—my friends and me—because we forgot he was, I don't know, a man? I'd like to know. I'd be embarrassed to ask, but I'd like to know.

We talk about this sometimes. I think Warren feels defensive. He knows there's a kind of innocence about most girls—they're girls, after all. The same behavior in a woman would be inexcusable. They'll find that out soon enough.

Meanwhile, I worry a little. I worry that one of those girls will naively put herself in a compromising position with some man who's less a man than my husband is.

And, sometimes—when things are hard at home and he's tired and stressed—sometimes I worry he'll be gripped by a desire that comes in the form of one of those little hardbodies who adores him.

It's not because I don't trust him. He's a wonderful man. But he's just a man, you know?

LIGHTS OUT.

discussion talk about it

Q: What grabbed you in Sarah's monologue?

Q: What do you think about her apprehensions?

Q: Without embarrassing anyone, have you seen what Sarah sees in the way girls treat men who make them feel safe? Talk about that.

Q: Sarah says most girls are innocent about this stuff in a naive way. What do you think about that?

Q: What can Warren do to head off trouble?

One youth worker said, "If I can't get a hip between me and a huggy girl, I'm not paying attention." What would you say to him?

Q: What would you tell Sarah if you were her friend?

What would you tell Warren?

What would you tell the kids in the youth group?

23

~~W+S:~~ WARREN SAYS HIS PIECE

[EPISODE 3]

WARREN is the youth worker in charge. He's married to Sarah; his age doesn't matter. Warren is half comic, half prophet, and half Greek chorus. Warren has a thing or two to say about a thing or two.

WARREN ADDRESSES THE AUDIENCE.

> **WARREN**
> I'm not cynical. I'm skeptical. There's a difference… You can trust me on this. I scored 1520 on the S.A.T.—weak math score.
>
> A *skeptic*, such as myself, tends to doubt the easy answer, the obvious explanation, the official story. The truth is, skeptics doubt just about everything we hear, especially if we're told it by an expert. And most especially if it's backed by statistics. Our favorite book title—it's a real book; look it up—our favorite book title is *How to Lie with Statistics*.
>
> The *cynic* is our natural enemy. This is because—hold on, I know what you're thinking: You're thinking one of two things. Either, "What a geek!" OR you're thinking, "Wait a minute! Isn't a cynic someone who believes people are motivated mainly by selfish motives?"
>
> Well, you're both right. But one of you is more right than the other.
>
> Because cynics believe people are motivated mainly by selfish motives, cynics will say whatever they think people want to hear. That's how they get what they want. That's their strategy, see? So, when I say this next thing, understand I'm not being cynical, okay? I'm being *skeptical*.

GOOD SEX DRAMA

Alright then, you ready? Here goes: I have yet to hear one credible story of unqualified success in the face of sexual temptation.

Oh, there are plenty of stories. I know that. I've told a few myself. I just don't believe any of them anymore. Least of all the ones I hear from experts. And preachers...preachers are right up there—guilty until proven innocent. Don't get me wrong: I believe they lie with the best intentions. They're only trying to protect the truth.

Go to any youth camp or conference and somebody will be doing a How to Overcome Sexual Temptation seminar. If it's a national conference, it's probably someone who goes from town to town, teaching the secrets of sexual purity. Again, don't get me wrong. I'm sure that person—they come in both male and female models—I'm convinced that person will be very nice and, most likely, quite entertaining. The presentation will include lots of stories, some video clips maybe, a few laughs, possibly even tears. It'll be a good show, almost certainly. And you'll want to sign the chastity pledge or make the purity promise or...*whatever*. You *will* because what they say will be right—or close enough—and *you* want to do the right thing, don't you? I do. I really want to do the right thing.

My problem is—see if you identify with this—my problem is, I keep failing to do the right thing.

On the positive side, I've had significant *success* at doing the wrong things. But I'm afraid my success may be canceled out by this pattern of failure to do the right thing...

Okay, I'm just goofin', but you see what I'm saying, don't you?

Stay with me now; it gets tricky here. For a long time I thought it was just me. I thought, "Hey, I'm the one who doesn't have what it takes so… Don't count on me." You know? "Count on someone else who _does_ have what it takes."

But then I started thinking—dangerous, I know—which led to even greater danger… I started reading the Bible…for _myself_.

Now hold on, because I know what you're thinking. You're thinking one of two things. Either: "It's that same geek who was talking before! What's his deal?" _OR_ you're thinking, "Wait a minute! Those seminar leaders read the Bible all the time. I _know_ they do. I've seen them do it with my own eyes."

And, of course, you're both right. But one of you is more right than the other.

Here's why—and remember now, I'm not a cynic, I'm a skeptic. The minute a seminar leader takes on the title _Seminar Leader_ he has something to lose. And when a national speaker goes out on the road, she's _really_ got something to lose. From this, you may guess why I'm skeptical about preachers—it's the same dilemma, isn't it?

Seminar leaders and sexual purity speakers—and preachers, too—have something to lose if they're not careful in what they say. At least that's how I imagine it must seem to them.

I mean, how do you think it would feel to not be invited back next time? How do you think it would feel to have to give the money back? How do you think it would feel to have your children in high school and, hopefully, on their way to college, and you have to start a new career and say, "Sorry kids, but you can't go to Westmont or Wheaton or any of those fine Christian schools that start with a W."

And the children would say, "Hey, Dad: what's the problem?"

And you would have to say, "Kids, I've been asked to resign my position at the church and move on." And they would say, "No way, Dad! You must have done something wrong. What did you do? Did you do something wrong?" And all you could say is, "No, I didn't do anything wrong. I just wasn't able to report unqualified success in the near term."… And of course your children would be upset and confused and they would say, "Dad, hey, tell us what you mean."

And all you could say—the whole of it—is, "Kids, I made the mistake of admitting a sexual temptation that is less than 20 years old."

Of course your children would shun you for a time, not so much because of the prestigious Christian colleges they couldn't attend, nor even for your lack of unqualified success against temptation in the near term. They would shun you because you were stupid enough to admit weakness. *You* know the rules: anything fresher than 20 years is just asking for it. It's just a good thing you're not running for public office. "You're *not* running for public office are you, Dad?"

Just imagine how that would feel. It wouldn't feel very good would it? So, naturally, most seminar leaders, sexual purity speakers, and everyday preachers do what's necessary to not feel those bad feelings. And, really, it's pretty simple. Just don't say anything. Or say *plenty*, but nothing that's not an unqualified success in the war against temptation. Old stories are fine. Anything 20 years out is acceptable as long as it's not too gross. Close calls are great storytelling. You can talk about close calls 'til the cows come home—as long as it's clear you were minding your own business when the trouble started.

Okay, see, I lost my way there for just a minute. Lessee...I was talking about reading the Bible for myself. Okay, lemme tell you what I found in the third chapter of the book of Romans; right after it says no one is righteous enough to be called holy based on his personal conduct. It says—

> This righteousness from God comes through faith in Jesus Christ to all who believe. There is no difference, for all have sinned and fall short of the glory of God, and are justified freely by his grace through the redemption that came by Christ Jesus.[3]

"_Oh!_" I said. I read that, and I said, "Wait a minute! Does that say _all_ have sinned and fall short of the glory of God? I believe that _is_ what it says." Which is interesting because I've gotten the impression that all fall short, but some of us fall farther shorter than others. I think you know who you are.

More to the point, I get the impression some people are better suited to be seminar leaders and sexual purity speakers and preachers than, say, the rest of us, because, while _everyone_ needs Jesus, a small number of folks apparently need Jesus somewhat less than, say, the rest of us, if you get my meaning.

Now, if you're one of those people who takes the Bible more or less seriously, you could have a problem with this. The Bible says—correct me if I'm wrong—_all_ have sinned.

All fall short of the glory of God. If we're trying to leap the Grand Canyon, I won't be much impressed if you jump farther than me. No matter how much canyon you clear, we'll still meet at the bottom. That's falling short.

[3]Romans 3:22-24

That said, it may be our fault some people are allowed to pretend they're more successful at resisting temptation than the rest of us. And by "our fault" I mean the fault of those who came before us, who supported the idea of an upper class of Christians who are somehow better than everyone else. And now we, like those before us, pay these people for representing themselves as the people we always wanted to be. And, honestly…? It's who they want to be as well.

Remember: I'm not cynical, I'm skeptical. I believe people who pretend they're better than others really want to _be_ better than others. Wait. That sounds bad. Let me try again. I believe they want to be better than _they_ are—as good as they allow us believe they are in their talks and books and videos.

I wish I could believe them.

C.S. Lewis wrote somewhere that no one knows how bad temptation can get except Jesus, because everyone _gives in_ so quickly—far too soon to grapple with the full-on fury of temptation at its extreme limits.

Except Jesus. Jesus found out how bad it can get—temptation—because Jesus fought it all the way to the end. The writer of the book of Hebrews says Jesus was tempted in every way everyone is tempted without ever once giving in. Not even once. So, Lewis figures, Jesus, of all people, knows how long temptation can go on and how bad it can get.

Do you see what I'm getting at? People who set themselves up as examples of virtue may just be asking for it. They may be painting targets on their chins, saying, "Go ahead. Hit me right here. Give it your best shot." That seems foolish to me but—S.A.T.s notwithstanding—what do I know?

Here's another possibility. Maybe those individuals haven't been much tempted in their area of expertise. I'm too young to remember this, but back in the 1980s First Lady Nancy Reagan sponsored an antidrug campaign called "Just Say No." It raised a lot of money, but the people it kept from using drugs were mainly people who weren't much interested in what drugs could do for them. I would have been one of those people. I don't much care about being drugged. Which is why I'm not qualified to speak to the issue of drug resistance.

I'm also not qualified to speak on the subject of shoplifting or cheating on tests because I've never been seriously tempted to do those things. I'd like to tell you that means I'm a virtuous person, but you see, I've _done_ everything I've been seriously tempted to do.

I'm not virtuous. Sooner or later, if I've been really tempted, I've buckled and, honestly, I thank God I'm not tempted to do some things that could get me thrown in jail, because I'm pretty sure—based on past experience— I'm pretty sure I would do those things. That's how _not virtuous_ I am.

I can speak to the temptations of greed and gluttony and lying and lust because I have a great deal of experience with these things. And I promise you, it wasn't 20 years ago.

I don't want to make you uncomfortable, but my last temptation to lust wasn't even 20 _minutes_ ago. I wish I could tell you I've defeated lust so often the Devil doesn't even bother me any more. But this is not the case.

Okay, now hold on because I know what you're thinking. You're thinking one of two things. You're thinking, "This geek never shuts up!" _OR_ you're thinking, "Wait a minute! If you take this to its logical conclusion, you're conceding defeat!" If two guys here in the back row were each thinking one of those thoughts, they'd both be right. But you know what? One would be more right than the other, and here's why: I _do_, in fact, concede defeat in the temptations that tempt _me_. I'm a truly needy person. _Still_. After all these years. So unless God joins the fight, I expect to lose. Oddly enough, I have a peaceful feeling about that, which, I believe, has more to do with God than me.

The rest of the temptations—the ones I'm not interested in?—hardly matter to me, and I have almost nothing to say about them.

So, see? Mr. Impatient-Head in the back row? I do shut up eventually. Stick a fork in me. I'm done.

LIGHTS OUT.

discussion talk about it

Q: What grabbed you about Warren's monologue?

Is there anything he said that's hard for you to buy? Talk about that.

Q: One way to interpret what Warren says is, "If someone seems too good to be true, that's because they are." What do you think about that?

Q: Warren claims no virtue for resisting impulses that aren't all that tempting to him. What's your response to his claim?

He also claims he's given in to everything that truly tempted him. What do you think about that?

Q: Do you agree with Warren that when we identify people as experts or leaders we make it difficult for them to tell the whole truth? Explain your thinking.

Q: Warren seems to have no problem admitting his need for God in the areas of lust and greed and glutton and lying. What do you make of that?

Some people would say a guy like Warren shouldn't be leading a group of kids. Do you agree or disagree? Explain.

Q: Warren thinks it's cynical for a writer or speaker who knows people are looking for hope to give the impression things are better than they really are. What do you think about that?

What do you think about communicators who give the impression their past was worse than it really was? Do you think that's cynical?

Q: Have you, like Warren, ever felt alone in your struggle with temptation? Talk about that.

Q: What do you think about C. S. Lewis' argument that Jesus knows more about temptation than anyone else because he resisted all the way to the end?

Take a look at I Corinthians 10:13. How does that play into this conversation?

Q: If Warren were here now, what question would you ask him or what statement would you make to him?

Q: If Jesus were here now, what question would you ask him or what statement would you make to him?

THE DREAM 24

The dream is delivered as free verse in which most lines follow quickly on the lines before them. Two characters on the same line speak in unison. Rehearse until you've established a fluid rhythm.

THE CHARACTERS—JULES, WARREN, GINNY, AND REPO—ADDRESS THE AUDIENCE. SPACE THEM UNEVENLY, ONE SITTING ON A CHAIR, ONE ON A TABLE, ONE STANDING ON THE FLOOR, ONE ON A SHORT STEP.

> **optional props...**
> **HANGING OUT STUFF**
> chair
> table

JULES
I had a dream about love.

WARREN
I had dream where no one thought love meant sex

GINNY
or sex meant love.

REPO
I had a dream where love meant giving

GINNY AND WARREN
not getting.

REPO
No one ever asked, "Did you get any?"

JULES
Because why would anyone say something so childish?

WARREN
"Did you get any?" <u>Sheesh</u>.

GINNY
In my dream, no one took advantage of anyone.

GOOD SEX DRAMA

REPO
Manipulation had nothing to do with sex.

WARREN
Force and sex were never used in the same sentence.

JULES
No one lied

REPO
or cheated.

WARREN
No one pretended

GINNY
or stole

JULES
for brief pleasure.

GINNY
No one ever used sex to hold on to another person

REPO
just a little longer.

WARREN
Everyone in my dream understood

GINNY
that sex is not an event

JULES
not an encounter

WARREN
not a flash in the pan.

REPO

In my dream, everyone understood that sex is relationship

GINNY

communication

JULES

commitment.

GINNY

I had a dream where there were no unintended pregnancies

JULES

because there was no unintentional sex.

WARREN

A dream where sex brought pleasure

REPO

but not just pleasure.

GINNY

Where sex was beautiful because it was whole

JULES

pure

REPO

devoted

WARREN

full of hope

GINNY

and truly safe.

WARREN

No one in my dream dreaded sex.

JULES

No one was confused about their sexuality.

REPO

No one ever used sex as a weapon

GINNY AND JULES

or a toy.

WARREN

And no one was ashamed in my dream.

REPO

No one was hurt

JULES

or confused

GINNY

or hobbled by regret

WARREN

because we understood love

JULES

and sex.

REPO

and sex.

WARREN

Every last one of us.

GINNY

Perfectly.

WARREN
I had this dream about love.

REPO
I don't think you'll be surprised to learn

JULES
I didn't wanna wake up.

LIGHTS OUT.

discussion talk about it

Q: What lines grabbed you in this piece?

Why do you think that's important?

Q: How do people understand the connection between love and sex in your world?

What are the outcomes of that understanding?

Q: Is it childish to ask, "Did you get any?" Explain your thoughts.

Q: Have you seen sex used as a weapon? Talk about that.

Have you seen sex used as a toy? Talk about that.

Have you seen sex used to hold on to someone? Talk about that.

Q: What would it take to make this dream a reality?

Resources from Youth Specialties

Ideas Library
Ideas Library on CD-ROM 2.0
Administration, Publicity, & Fundraising
Camps, Retreats, Missions, & Service Ideas
Creative Meetings, Bible Lessons, & Worship Ideas
Crowd Breakers & Mixers
Discussion & Lesson Starters
Discussion & Lesson Starters 2
Drama, Skits, & Sketches
Drama, Skits, & Sketches 2
Drama, Skits, & Sketches 3
Games
Games 2
Games 3
Holiday Ideas
Special Events

Bible Curricula
Creative Bible Lessons from the Old Testament
Creative Bible Lessons in 1 & 2 Corinthians
Creative Bible Lessons in Galatians and Philippians
Creative Bible Lessons in John
Creative Bible Lessons in Romans
Creative Bible Lessons on the Life of Christ
Creative Bible Lessons in Psalms
Downloading the Bible Kit
Wild Truth Bible Lessons
Wild Truth Bible Lessons 2
Wild Truth Bible Lessons—Pictures of God

Topical Curricula
Creative Junior High Programs from A to Z, Vol. 1 (A-M)
Creative Junior High Programs from A to Z, Vol. 2 (N-Z)
Girls: 10 Gutsy, God-Centered Sessions on Issues That Matter to Girls
Guys: 10 Fearless, Faith-Focused Sessions on Issues That Matter to Guys
Good Sex
Live the Life! Student Evangelism Training Kit
The Next Level Youth Leader's Kit
Roaring Lambs
So What Am I Gonna Do with My Life?
Student Leadership Training Manual
Student Underground
Talking the Walk
What Would Jesus Do? Youth Leader's Kit
Wild Truth Bible Lessons
Wild Truth Bible Lessons 2
Wild Truth Bible Lessons—Pictures of God

Discussion Starters
Discussion & Lesson Starters (Ideas Library)
Discussion & Lesson Starters 2 (Ideas Library)
EdgeTV
Every Picture Tells a Story
Get 'Em Talking
Good Sex Drama
Keep 'Em Talking!
High School TalkSheets—Updated!
More High School TalkSheets—Updated!
High School TalkSheets from Psalms and Proverbs—Updated!
Junior High-Middle School TalkSheets—Updated!
More Junior High-Middle School TalkSheets—Updated!
Junior High-Middle School TalkSheets from Psalms and Proverbs—Updated!
Real Kids Ultimate Discussion Starting Video:
    Castaways
    Growing Up Fast
    Hardship & Healing
    Quick Takes
    Survivors
    Word on the Street
Small Group Qs
Have You Ever...?
Name Your Favorite
Unfinished Sentences
What If...?
Would You Rather...?

Drama Resources
Drama, Skits, & Sketches (Ideas Library)
Drama, Skits, & Sketches 2 (Ideas Library)
Drama, Skits, & Sketches 3 (Ideas Library)
Dramatic Pauses
Good Sex Drama
Spontaneous Melodramas
Spontaneous Melodramas 2
Super Sketches for Youth Ministry

Game Resources
Games (Ideas Library)
Games 2 (Ideas Library)
Games 3 (Ideas Library)
Junior High Game Nights
More Junior High Game Nights
Play It!
Screen Play CD-ROM

Additional Programming Resources
(also see Discussion Starters)
Camps, Retreats, Missions, & Service Ideas (Ideas Library)
Creative Meetings, Bible Lessons, & Worship Ideas (Ideas Library)
Crowd Breakers & Mixers (Ideas Library)
Everyday Object Lessons
Great Fundraising Ideas for Youth Groups
More Great Fundraising Ideas for Youth Groups
Great Retreats for Youth Groups
Great Talk Outlines for Youth Ministry
Holiday Ideas (Ideas Library)
Incredible Questionnaires for Youth Ministry
Kickstarters
Memory Makers
Special Events (Ideas Library)
Videos That Teach
Videos That Teach 2
Worship Services for Youth Groups

Quick Question Books
Have You Ever...?
Name Your Favorite
Small Group Qs
Unfinished Sentences
What If...?
Would You Rather...?

Videos & Video Curricula
Dynamic Communicators Workshop
EdgeTV
Live the Life! Student Evangelism Training Kit
Make 'Em Laugh!
Purpose-Driven® Youth Ministry Training Kit
Real Kids Ultimate Discussion Starting Video:
    Castaways
    Growing Up Fast
    Hardship & Healing
    Quick Takes
    Survivors
    Word on the Street
Student Underground
Understanding Your Teenager Video Curriculum
Youth Ministry Outside the Lines

Especially for Junior High
Creative Junior High Programs from A to Z, Vol. 1 (A-M)
Creative Junior High Programs from A to Z, Vol. 2 (N-Z)
Junior High Game Nights
More Junior High Game Nights
JuniorHigh-Middle School TalkSheets—Updated!
More Junior High-Middle School TalkSheets—Updated!
Junior High-Middle School TalkSheets from Psalms and Proverbs—Updated!
Wild Truth Journal for Junior Highers
Wild Truth Bible Lessons
Wild Truth Bible Lessons 2
Wild Truth Journal—Pictures of God
Wild Truth Bible Lessons—Pictures of God

Student Resources
Downloading the Bible: A Rough Guide to the New Testament
Downloading the Bible: A Rough Guide to the Old Testament
Grow for It! Journal through the Scriptures
So What Am I Gonna Do with My Life?
Spiritual Challenge Journal: The Next Level
Teen Devotional Bible
What (Almost) Nobody Will Tell You about Sex
What Would Jesus Do? Spiritual Challenge Journal

Clip Art
Youth Group Activities (print)
Clip Art Library Version 2.0 (CD-ROM)

Digital Resources
Clip Art Library Version 2.0 (CD-ROM)
Great Talk Outlines for Youth Ministry
Hot Illustrations CD-ROM
Ideas Library on CD-ROM 2.0
Screen Play
Youth Ministry Management Tools

Professional Resources
Administration, Publicity, & Fundraising (Ideas Library)
Dynamic Communicators Workshop
Great Talk Outlines for Youth Ministry
Help! I'm a Junior High Youth Worker!
Help! I'm a Small-Group Leader!
Help! I'm a Sunday School Teacher!
Help! I'm an Urban Youth Worker!
Help! I'm a Volunteer Youth Worker!
Hot Illustrations for Youth Talks
Just Shoot Me: A Practical Guide for Using Your Video Camera in Youth Ministry
More Hot Illustrations for Youth Talks
Still More Hot Illustrations for Youth Talks
Hot Illustrations for Youth Talks 4
How to Expand Your Youth Ministry
How to Speak to Youth...and Keep Them Awake at the Same Time
Junior High Ministry (Updated & Expanded)
Make 'Em Laugh!
The Ministry of Nurture
Postmodern Youth Ministry
Purpose-Driven® Youth Ministry
Purpose-Driven® Youth Ministry Training Kit
So *That's* Why I Keep Doing This!
Teaching the Bible Creatively
A Youth Ministry Crash Course
Youth Ministry Management Tools
The Youth Worker's Handbook to Family Ministry

Academic Resources
Four Views of Youth Ministry & the Church
Starting Right
Youth Ministry That Transforms